# SMITH
## WIGGLESWORTH
### ON
# HEAVEN

## GOD'S GREAT PLAN FOR YOUR LIFE

w

WHITAKER
HOUSE

Whitaker House gratefully acknowledges and thanks Glenn Gohr and the entire staff of the Assemblies of God Archives in Springfield, Missouri, for graciously assisting us in compiling Smith Wigglesworth's works for publication in this book.

Unless otherwise indicated, all Scripture quotations are taken from the *New King James Version,* © 1979, 1980, 1982 by Thomas Nelson, Inc. Used by permission. All rights reserved. Scripture quotations marked (KJV) are taken from the King James Version of the Holy Bible.

*Publisher's note:* The compiled works in this book from Whitaker House have been updated for today's reader. Words, expressions, and sentence structure have been revised for clarity and readability. Although the NKJV translation was not available to Smith Wigglesworth, this Bible version was prayerfully selected in order to make the language of the entire text readily understandable while maintaining the author's original premises and message.

## SMITH WIGGLESWORTH ON HEAVEN:
### God's Great Plan for Your Life

(previously published under the title
*Smith Wigglesworth on God's Transforming Power*)

ISBN: 0-88368-954-5
Printed in the United States of America
© 1998 by Whitaker House

Whitaker House
30 Hunt Valley Circle
New Kensington, PA 15068
www.whitakerhouse.com

**Library of Congress Cataloging-in-Publication Data**

Wigglesworth, Smith, 1859–1947.
[Smith Wigglesworth on God's transforming power]
Smith Wigglesworth on heaven : God's great plan for your life /
Smith Wigglesworth.
p.   cm.
Originally published: Smith Wigglesworth on God's transforming  power.
© 1998.
ISBN 0-88368-954-5 (trade pbk. : alk. paper)
1. Spiritual life—Pentecostal churches. 2. Heaven. I. Title.
BV4501.3.W5423 2003
252'.0994—dc22
2003015785

2 3  4  5  6  7  8  9  10  11  12   **UJ**   11  10  09  08  07  06  05  04

# Contents

# Introduction

n encounter with Smith Wigglesworth was an unforgettable experience. This seems to be the universal reaction of all who knew him or heard him speak. Smith Wigglesworth was a simple yet remarkable man who was used in an extraordinary way by our extraordinary God. He had a contagious and inspiring faith. Under his ministry, thousands of people came to salvation, committed themselves to a deeper faith in Christ, received the baptism in the Holy Spirit, and were miraculously healed. The power that brought these kinds of results was the presence of the Holy Spirit, who filled Smith Wigglesworth and used him in bringing the good news of the Gospel to people all over the world. Wigglesworth gave glory to God for everything that was accomplished through his ministry, and he wanted people to understand his work only in this context, because his sole desire was that people would see Jesus and not himself.

Smith Wigglesworth was born in England in 1859. Immediately after his conversion as a boy, he had a concern for the salvation of others and won people to Christ, including his mother. Even so, as a young man, he could not express himself well enough to give a testimony in church, much less preach a sermon. Wigglesworth said that his mother had the same difficulty in expressing herself that he did. This family trait, coupled with the fact that he had no formal education because he began working twelve hours a day at the age of seven to help support the family, contributed to Wigglesworth's awkward speaking style. He became a plumber by trade, yet he continued to devote himself to winning many people to Christ on an individual basis.

In 1882, he married Polly Featherstone, a vivacious young woman who loved God and had a gift of preaching and evangelism. It was she who taught him to read and who became his closest confidant and strongest supporter. They both had compassion for the poor and needy in their community, and they opened a mission, at which Polly preached. Significantly, people were miraculously healed when Wigglesworth prayed for them.

In 1907, Wigglesworth's circumstances changed dramatically when, at the age of forty-eight, he was baptized in the Holy Spirit. Suddenly, he had a new power that enabled him to preach, and even his wife was amazed at the transformation. This was the beginning of what became a worldwide evangelistic and healing ministry that reached thousands. He eventually ministered in the United States, Australia, South Africa, and all over Europe. His ministry extended up to the time of his death in 1947.

Several emphases in Smith Wigglesworth's life and ministry characterize him: a genuine, deep compassion for the unsaved and sick; an unflinching belief in the Word of God; a desire that Christ should increase and he should decrease (John 3:30); a belief that he was called to exhort people to enlarge their

# Introduction

faith and trust in God; an emphasis on the baptism in the Holy Spirit with the manifestation of the gifts of the Spirit as in the early church; and a belief in complete healing for everyone of all sickness.

Smith Wigglesworth was called "The Apostle of Faith" because absolute trust in God was a constant theme of both his life and his messages. In his meetings, he would quote passages from the Word of God and lead lively singing to help build people's faith and encourage them to act on it. He emphasized belief in the fact that God could do the impossible. He had great faith in what God could do, and God did great things through him.

Wigglesworth's unorthodox methods were often questioned. As a person, Wigglesworth was reportedly courteous, kind, and gentle. However, he became forceful when dealing with the devil, whom he believed caused all sickness. Wigglesworth said the reason he spoke bluntly and acted forcefully with people was that he knew he needed to get their attention so they could focus on God. He also had such anger toward the devil and sickness that he acted in a seemingly rough way. When he prayed for people to be healed, he would often hit or punch them at the place of their problem or illness. Yet, no one hurt by this startling treatment. Instead, they were remarkably healed. When he was asked why he treated people in this manner, he said that he was not hitting the people but that he was hitting the devil. He believed that Satan should never be treated gently or allowed to get away with anything. About twenty people were reportedly raised from the dead after he prayed for them. Wigglesworth himself was healed of appendicitis and kidney stones, after which his personality softened and he was more gentle with those who came to him for prayer for healing. His abrupt manner in ministering may be attributed to the fact that he was very serious about his calling and got down to business quickly.

Although Wigglesworth believed in complete healing, he encountered illnesses and deaths that were difficult to understand. These included the deaths of his wife and son, his daughter's lifelong deafness, and his own battles with kidney stones and sciatica.

He often seemed paradoxical: compassionate but forceful, blunt but gentle, a well-dressed gentleman whose speech was often ungrammatical or confusing. However, he loved God with everything he had, he was steadfastly committed to God and to His Word, and he didn't rest until he saw God move in the lives of those who needed Him.

In 1936, Smith Wigglesworth prophesied about what we now know as the charismatic movement. He accurately predicted that the established mainline denominations would experience revival and the gifts of the Spirit in a way that would surpass even the Pentecostal movement. Wigglesworth did not live to see the renewal, but as an evangelist and prophet with a remarkable healing ministry, he had a tremendous influence on both the Pentecostal and charismatic movements, and his example and influence on believers is felt to this day.

Without the power of God that was so obviously present in his life and ministry, we might not be reading transcripts of his sermons, for his spoken messages were often disjointed and ungrammatical. However, true gems of spiritual insight shine

# Introduction

through them because of the revelation he received through the Holy Spirit. It was his life of complete devotion and belief in God and his reliance on the Holy Spirit that brought the life-changing power of God into his messages.

As you read this book, it is important to remember that Wigglesworth's works span a period of several decades, from the early 1900s to the 1940s. They were originally presented as spoken rather than written messages, and necessarily retain some of the flavor of a church service or prayer meeting. Some of the messages were Bible studies that Wigglesworth led at various conferences. At his meetings, he would often speak in tongues and give the interpretation, and these messages have been included as well. Because of Wigglesworth's unique style, the sermons and Bible studies in this book have been edited for clarity, and archaic expressions that would be unfamiliar to modern readers have been updated.

In conclusion, we hope that as you read these words of Smith Wigglesworth, you will truly sense his complete trust and unwavering faith in God and take to heart one of his favorite sayings: "Only believe!"

# One

# Preparing for Christ's Return

od has a plan for us that is greater than our thoughts, greater than words can say, and so I am not frightened of beginning with a sort of spiritual exaggeration. I dare to believe that God will help me to say things to you that will inspire you to dare to believe God.

Up to this present time, the Lord's word for us has been, *"Until now you have asked nothing"* (John 16:24). Surely you who have been asking great things from God for a long time would be amazed if you entered into it with clear knowledge that it is the Master, it is Jesus, who has such knowledge of the mightiness of the power of the Father and of the joint union with Him, that nothing is impossible for you to ask. Surely it is He alone who could say, *"Until now you have asked nothing."*

God wants me to press you another step further. Begin to believe on extravagant asking, believing that God is pleased when you ask large things.

If you will only dispose of yourself—for it is nothing but yourself that will hinder you—it may be today that God will so transform you that you will be an altogether different person, as you have never been before. Get rid of your human mind, get rid of your human measure, get rid of your strength, and get rid of all you have—this is a big thing for me to say—and let inspiration take charge of you entirely, and bring you out of yourself into the power of God.

### Interpretation of Tongues

Only the divine mind has divine thought to meet human order, for knowing us from the beginning and understanding us as a Father and pitying us as children, He begins with the blade and the head and the full grain in the head. He does this so that we might know that He won't take us out of our death, but He will transform us moment by moment until we can come into full stature of the mind and thought and prayer and action. Hallelujah! God is on the throne.

Now, beloved in the Lord, I want to inspire you to believe that this day is for you as a beginning of days. You have never passed this way before. So I bring you to another day of passing over any heights, passing through mists or darkness. Dare to believe that the cloud is upon you, and it will break with an exceeding reward of blessing. Don't be afraid of clouds—they are all earthly. Never be afraid of an earthly thing. You belong to a higher order, a divine order, a spiritual order. Then believe that God wants you to soar high this day.

### Interpretation of Tongues

Fear not to enter in, for the Lord your God has you now in preparation. He is proving you, and He is chastising you, but His hand is

not heavy upon you as you may think, for He is
gentle and entreating to bring you into the desired place of your heart's affections.

"*Be still, and know that I am God'* (Ps.
46:10). It is I and I alone who opens to you the
good treasure."

Oh, to be still, that my mind may be so
free from the cares of this life that I might be
able to enter into the joy and the bliss God has
caused me to, for I have not passed this way
until now!

God is going to speak to us about entering into
something we have not entered into before.

## Living in Perfect Readiness

The thoughts of this message are primary to the
message of the coming of the Lord. There must be a
place of preparation and a line of understanding, because of the purposes that God is arranging for us. I
know He is at the door. Spiritual perception makes us
know of His near return. But we must be so built on
the line of truth that when He comes we are ready.

I am going to tell you about the revelation of
Christ to me of the readiness, and what it is—the
knowledge of it, the power of it, the purpose of it—
until every vestige of our beings is so filled with it
that it would be impossible for us to be out of it. We
will be in the midst of it.

I have a message leading up to the knowledge of
His coming. It is in Peter's second epistle:

*Knowing this first: that scoffers will come in
the last days, walking according to their own
lusts, and saying, "Where is the promise of His*

15

*coming? For since the fathers fell asleep, all things continue as they were from the beginning of creation." For this they willfully forget: that by the word of God the heavens were of old, and the earth standing out of water and in the water, by which the world that then existed perished, being flooded with water. But the heavens and the earth which are now preserved by the same word, are reserved for fire until the day of judgment and perdition of ungodly men. But, beloved, do not forget this one thing, that with the Lord one day is as a thousand years, and a thousand years as one day. The Lord is not slack concerning His promise, as some count slackness, but is longsuffering toward us, not willing that any should perish but that all should come to repentance. But the day of the Lord will come as a thief in the night, in which the heavens will pass away with a great noise, and the elements will melt with fervent heat; both the earth and the works that are in it will be burned up. Therefore, since all these things will be dissolved, what manner of persons ought you to be in holy conduct and godliness, looking for and hastening the coming of the day of God, because of which the heavens will be dissolved, being on fire, and the elements will melt with fervent heat? Nevertheless we, according to His promise, look for new heavens and a new earth in which righteousness dwells. Therefore, beloved, looking forward to these things, be diligent to be found by Him in peace, without spot and blameless; and consider that the longsuffering of our Lord is salvation.* (2 Pet. 3:3–15)

# Preparing for Christ's Return

I may deal with many things on the line of spiritual awakening, for this is what is needed this day. This day is a needy day of spiritual awakening, not so much as a knowledge of salvation but a knowledge of waking in salvation.

The seed of the Lord Jesus Christ is mightily in you. This seed is a seed of purifying, a seed of truth and knowledge, a seed of life-giving, a seed of transforming, a seed of building another person in the body until the body that bears the seed only lives to contain the body that the seed has made. Then, that seed comes forth with glorious light and power until the whole body has yielded itself to another, to a fullness, to a manifestation of the perfect formation of the Christ in you. This is the great hope of the future day.

I want to speak to you very exactly. All the people who are pressing into and getting ready for this glorious, attained place where they will not be found naked, where they will be blameless, where they will be immovable, where they will be purified by the power of the Word of God, have within them a consciousness of the very presence of God. They know that God is working within them, changing their very nature and preparing them for a greater thing and causing them to be ready for translation.

## The World Is Ripening for Judgment

You will find that this thing is not already in the world in perfection. There are millions and millions of real believers in Christ who are losing this great upward look, and in the measure they lose this upward look, they lose perfect purification.

There is only perfect purification in looking upward to God.

When we see the Day dawning as *"the manifestation of the sons of God"* (Rom. 8:19 KJV) appears, just as these things come to us in light and revelation, we will find that it makes us know that everything is decaying. Millions of people who are Christians believe this world is being purified. All the saints of God who get the real vision of this wonderful transformation of the body are seeing every day that the world is getting worse and worse and worse and is ripening for Judgment. God is bringing us to a place where we who are spiritual are having a clear vision that we must, at any cost, put off the works of darkness; we must be getting ourselves ready for the glorious Day.

These are the last days. What will be the strongest confirmation of the last days?

There are in the world two classes of believers. There are believers who are disobedient—or I ought to say there are children who are saved by the power of God, but who are disobedient children—and there are children who are also saved by the power of God who are longing to be more obedient all the time.

In this factor, Satan has a great part to play. It is on this factor in these last years that some of us have been brought to great grief at the first opening of the door to carnal forces. We heard the word come rushing through all over—"new theology," that damnable, devilish, evil power that lived in some of these disobedient children who in these last days opened the door to the next new thing.

As soon as this new theology was noised abroad everywhere, everybody began to say, "What is new theology?" Why, new theology is exactly on the same level as the idea that men came from monkeys. What does it mean? I want to make a clean sweep of it. There is not a man who can think on those lines and not also think on the lines of atheism. Every person who touches a thing like that is an atheist behind all he has to say.

New theology was born in infidelity; it is atheism, and it opened the door for the early Jehovah's Witnesses, whose religion is full of false prophecy. Take a look at their beliefs, and go into the prophecy. What was the prophecy? In 1924 the prophecy was that the Lord would return. Jehovah's Witnesses hold false prophecy. Their belief system is exactly the perfect plan that will make the Man of Sin come forth. The Jehovah's Witnesses are preparing the door for the Man of Sin, and they are receiving openheartedly.

They had also declared that Jesus would come in 1914. I went to see a dear beloved brother of mine who was so deluded by this false prophecy that he was utterly deceived by it. I said, "You will be deceived as sure as you live."

He replied, "We are so sure it is true that if we are deceived we will give up all Jehovah's Witness beliefs and have nothing to do with them."

But what does false prophecy do? False prophecy always makes a way out. The moment it did not come to pass, the Jehovah's Witnesses said that they were mistaken in dates. That is the devil. If it had been a true prophecy, Jesus would have come. And the Word of God says that if any prophecy does not come true, the prophet who spoke it has to prophesy no more.

But those people were deluded by the spirit of this world, the devil, and instantly they allowed themselves to be gripped by it again. And the same prophet came forth saying that Christ was going to come in 1925.

In order to cover that, what did they do? They announced in almost every nation, in the big cities, the words, "Millions are alive who will never die," and they have been going at that now since 1925. They are dying all the time; their prophecy is still a cursed, evil prophecy, yet they go on.

The spirit of this age is to get you to believe a lie. If you believe a lie, you cannot believe the truth. When once you are seasoned with a lie against the Word of God, He sends you strong delusion so that you will believe a lie. Who sends it? God does. God is gracious over His Word. His Word is from everlasting; His Word is true.

When we see these things that are coming to pass, what do we know? We know the time is at hand. The fig tree is budding for these false prophecies and these positions.

Now, you see, they never stop at that. They go on to say Christ never has risen. Of course, if you ever believe a lie, if you ever turn from the Word of God to some other place, you cannot believe the truth after that.

## Warding Off Evil

Then the last days opened the door for that false demon power that is rampant everywhere in the world. This power is putting up the most marvelous buildings, including that of Christian Science, which is devilish, hellish, and deceiving. I am preaching to you this morning so that you will deliver yourself from this present-day evil. How will you do it? You can do it only on one line. Let the seed in. Let in the seed of truth, the seed of righteousness, this power of God, this inward incorruptible.

The seed of Christ is an inward incorruptible. The new birth, the new life, is a quickening power; it is incorruptible, dealing with corruptible, carnal, evil, sensuous, devilish things. And when it comes to the Word of God, the seed of the Word of God is the life of the Word, and you are living the life of the Word of God and are tremendously transformed all the time by the Word of the Lord.

These are the last days. You go out in the world, and there is no difficulty. What are you going to do now? Is this a fact? Is this true? Aren't people today almost afraid of sending their sons and daughters to the colleges and universities, because they come out more like devils than they were when they went in? Isn't atheism right in the seat of almost all these colleges? Then what should you do? How will you keep your soul in peace? How will you preserve your children? How will you help them? You say they have to go because you want them to come out with certain degrees to their names; you want them to progress in knowledge, but how will you save your children?

Nothing but the Word can save them.

I wish all the young people in this place would read these words in the second epistle of John: *"Young men...you are strong...and you have overcome the wicked one"* (1 John 2:14). By what have they overcome? By the Word.

These are mighty words we read in this Scripture. What does it say?

## The Power of Revelation

The Word is holding these things, even the fires that are going to burn up all the world. The Word is holding them. What is the Word? The Word is the mighty power of the revelation to us of the Son of God. And the Son of God is holding all these powers today in the world, ready for the greatest conflagration that ever could be, when the heavens will be burned up, when the earth will melt with fervent heat (2 Pet. 3:10).

The Word of God is keeping these things reserved and all ready. What manner of men ought we to be? We ought to be purifying ourselves in all our actions. (See verse 11.)

Remember this about heaven: the glory, the revelation, the power, the presence, and all that makes heaven so full of beauty, is that time has no meaning there. It is so lovely; a thousand years are as a day, and a day as a thousand years (v. 8).

## Interpretation of Tongues

All the springs are in you (Ps. 87:7), all the revelations are in your midst. It is He, the mighty God! It is He, the King of Kings! It is He, the Son of the living God, who is in the very innermost being of your human nature, making you to know that, before these things will come to pass, you will be preserved in the midst of the flame. Whatever happens, God will cover you with His mighty covering; and that which is in you is incorruptible and undefiled and does not fade away, which is reserved in the glory.

God says to us, *"By your patience possess your souls"* (Luke 21:19). How beautiful! Oh, how the enrichment of the presence of the power of the Most High is bursting forth upon our—what can I say?—our human frames. No, it is something greater than the human frame. Do you not know that what is born in you is greater than anything formed around you? Do you not know that He who has been begotten in you is the very God of power to preserve you and to bring forth light and truth and cause the vision to be made clearer?

## The Elect of God

Take note of this: there is an elect of God. I know that God has in this place people who are the elect of God, and if you would examine yourself, you would be amazed to find that you are one of them. People are tremendously afraid of this position because they have so often heard, "Oh, you know you are the elect of God! You are sure to be all right." There have been great churches in England that were founded upon these things. I thank God that they have all withered. If you go to England, you will find that those strong people who used to hold all these things are almost withered out. Why? Because they went on to say that, if you were elect, you were right in whatever you did. That is wrong.

The elect of God are those who are pressing forward. The elect of God cannot hold still: they are always on the wing. Every person who has any knowledge of the elect of God realizes it is important that he press forward. He cannot endure sin or darknesses or shady things. The elect are so in earnest to be elect for God that they burn every bridge behind them.

Know that first there will be a falling away (2 Thess. 2:3). God will bring into His treasury the realities of the truth and put them side by side: the false, the true; those that can be shaken, and those that cannot be shaken. God wants us to be so built upon the foundation of truth that we cannot be shaken in our minds, no matter what comes.

## The Man of Sin

When I was in Sydney, they said, "Whatever you do, you must see this place that they built for the man, the new man who is coming."

Theosophy, which is based on theories of reincarnation and other falsities, has a new man. Nothing but Theosophy could have a new man. The foundation of this Theosophy has always been corruptible. From the beginning, it has been corruptible. In the formation of Theosophy, it was connected to one of the greatest atheists of the day; so you can only expect Theosophy to be atheism. It sprang out of atheism.

The Man of Sin, as he comes forth, will do many things. There will be many false christs, and they will be manifestations of the forthcoming of the Man of Sin, but they will all come to an end. The Man of Sin will be made manifest.

These people are determined to have a man. They know someone has to come. We Christians know who

# Preparing for Christ's Return

He is who is coming to us. But these people begin to make a man in this manner: they find a man in India, they polish him up as much as they can, and they make him as—well, in appearance they dress him up, but we are told by the Lord that soft clothing can go onto wolves' backs (Matt. 7:15).

We find that they are going to bring this man forth in great style. When I went around the amphitheater in Sydney that was made for this man to come, I saw as clearly as anything it was the preparation for the Man of Sin. But they do not believe that.

What will make you to know it is the Man of Sin? This: every religious sect and creed that are in the world all join to it. There is not a religion known that has not joined up to it.

Why, that is exactly what the devil wants. He wants all the false religions joining right up, and the Man of Sin will be received with great applause when he comes.

Who will be saved? Who will know the day? Who now knows the Man of Sin? We feel him when we touch him, when he opens his mouth, when he writes through the paper, when we see his actions—we know who he is.

What has the Man of Sin always said? Why, exactly what Jehovah's Witnesses say. What? That there is no hell. The devil has always said that. What does Christian Science say? No hell, no devil. They are ready for him. The devil has always said no hell, no evil. And these people are preparing, though they do not know it, for the Man of Sin.

We have to see that these days have to come before the Lord can come. There has to be a falling away. There has to be in this day a manifestation so clear, of such undeniable fact. I tell you, when they begin to build temples for the Man of Sin to come (though they don't know it), you know the Day is at hand.

A person said to me, "You see, the Christian Scientists must be right. Look at the beautiful buildings; look at all the people following them." Yes, everybody can belong to it. You can go to any brothel you like, you can go to any theater you like, you can go to any race course you like, you can be mixed up with the rest of the people in your life and still be a Christian Scientist. You can have the devil right and left and anywhere and still belong to Christian Science.

When the Man of Sin comes, he will be hailed on all sides. When he is manifested, who will miss him? Why, the reverent, the holy, the separated will miss him. Why will they miss him? Because they will not be here to greet him!

## Ready for Christ's Return

But there will be things that will happen prior to his coming that we will know. You can tell. I am like one this morning who is moving with a liquid, holy, indispensable, real fire in my bosom, and I know it is burning and the body is not consumed.

It is real fire from heaven that is making my utterances come to you to know that Christ is coming; He is on the way. God is going to help me tell you why you will know. You who have the breath of the Spirit, there is something moving now as I speak. As I speak, this breath of mighty, quickening, moving, changing, desirable power is making you to know, and it is this alone that is making you know that you will be ready.

No matter who else misses it, you will be ready. This is what I want to press upon you today, so that you will be ready. And you won't question your position. You will know. Ah, thank God, you are not of the night; you are of the day (1 Thess. 5:5). Christ's coming will not overtake you as a thief. You are the children of the day. You are not children of the night; you are not drunken. People are drunken in the night. You are not drunken. Oh, yes, you are. There is so much intoxication from this holy incarnation that makes you feel all the time you have to have Him hold you up. Praise the Lord! Holy intoxication, inspired revelation, invocation, incessantly inwardly moving your very nature, so that you know sure as anything that you do not belong to those who are putting off the day. You are hastening unto the Day; you are longing for day.

You say, "What a great Day!" Why do you say it? Because the creature inside the temple longs, travails, groans to be delivered, and will be delivered. Is this body the creature? No. This is the temple that holds the creature. It is the living creature. It is the new creature. It is the new creation. It is the new nature. It is the new life.

What manner of men ought we to be? *"The Lord is not slack concerning His promise, as some count slackness, but is longsuffering toward us, not willing that any should perish but that all should come to repentance"* (2 Pet. 3:9). I want you to notice this: this is not referring to the wicked who have repented. The epistles are always directed toward the

27

saints of God. When I speak to you saints of God, you will find that my language will make you see that there is not within you one thing that has to be covered. I say it without fear of contradiction, because it is my whole life and is inspired by the Truth. You know that these things will purify you.

## A Spiritual Teaching

It is on this line that you hear people speak. I do not mean it as a theory. This is not a theory. There is a great difference between a man standing before you on theory and one who stands on spiritual knowledge. The man of theory has chapter and verse, line upon line, precept upon precept (see Isaiah 28:13), and he works it out upon the scriptural basis. It is wonderful, it is good, it is inspiring; but I am not there. Mine is another approach. Mine is the spiritual nature showing you that the world is ripening for Judgment. Mine is a spiritual acquaintance bringing you to a place of separation and holiness unto God, so that you may purify yourself and be clean, ready for the great Day.

This is the day of purifying; this is the day of holiness; this is the day of separation; this is the day of waking. Oh, God, let us wake today! Let our inner spirits wake into consciousness that God is calling us. The Lord is upon us. We see that the Day is upon us. We look at the left side, we look at the right side, we see everywhere new theories. New things will not stand the light of the truth. When you see these things, you know there must be a great falling away before the Day. And it is coming; it is upon us.

Paul said he travailed in birth so that Christ might be formed in the saints (Gal. 4:19). Jesus did

# Preparing for Christ's Return

the same, and John did the same. So, brothers and sisters, may God bless you and make you see that this is a day of travailing for the church of God, that she might be formed in readiness for putting on the glorious raiment of heaven forever and forever.

> *Therefore, since all these things will be dissolved, what manner of persons ought you to be in holy conduct and godliness, looking for and hastening the coming of the day of God, because of which the heavens will be dissolved, being on fire, and the elements will melt with fervent heat? Nevertheless we, according to His promise, look for new heavens and a new earth in which righteousness dwells. Therefore, beloved, looking forward to these things, be diligent to be found by Him in peace, without spot and blameless.* (2 Pet. 3:11–14)

*"Without spot and blameless."* Do you believe it? What can do this for us? Only the blood of Jesus can do it. Oh, the blood of the Lamb! The blood of Jesus can do it. It can make us spotless, clean, and preserved for God.

Give the devil the biggest chase of his life, and say these words: *"The blood of Jesus Christ* [God's] *Son cleanses us from all sin"* (1 John 1:7).

If you ever hear something about the blood of Jesus in any Christian Science meeting, come tell me, and I will tell you that they are being converted. If you ever hear talk of Jehovah's Witnesses getting excited over the blood of Jesus, I can tell you that God has dealt with them. If ever you hear about this new leader in Theosophy getting excited about the blood of Jesus, you can tell them from

29

Wigglesworth that there is a new order in the world. But they have no room for the blood of Christ. And yet we see the blood is preparing us for this great Day.

In that amphitheater in Sydney, when I spoke about the blood and when I spoke about this infernal thing, the whole place was upset. Be careful when anybody comes to you with a sugar-coated pill or with a slimy tongue. They are always of the devil. The Spirit of the Lord will always deal with truth. These people never deal with truth. They always cover up the truth. They say, "Oh, you can be sure that we are all sons of God; we all belong to God." That is what people said when Jesus was here, and He said, "You are mistaken: you belong to the devil" (John 8:44). And if Jesus dared to say things like that, I dare.

## Questions Answered

**Q:** Is it true if we believe a lie we cannot believe the truth?

**A:** That is not what I said. As soon as you believe the Word of God to be a lie, then you cannot believe the truth of the Word of God. The Word of God comes to you like life and revelation; but Satan in his spurious condition comes, as he has done with many, and moves you from believing in truth to believing in some theory of truth. Once Satan has this hold on people, they have a theory of something else that is not truth, and they have denied the truth to take hold of the theory. It is all theory when people have left the truth. The people who live in truth never have a theory; it is always fact.

## Preparing for Christ's Return

**Q:** Because I have laid aside my Christian Science books, people are now using what they call "malicious magnetism" against me. I know Jesus is stronger than they.

**A:** This is a very important thing. There are many people so under delusion and so oppressed by the devil on these lines that they join together to damage the character of others because they do not go their way. That is the devil if nothing else is. The greatest fact about Christian Science's false position is that its followers are led captive by the Father of Lies. He has been a liar from the beginning. They have stepped out of truth and have been taken by this monster the devil until they cannot believe the truth.

Jesus said, "*'I am the light of the world. He who follows Me shall not walk in darkness'* (John 8:12). I am the light *'which gives light to every man coming into the world'* (John 1:9)."

If you will go back to the time when you knew that the light of the truth was burning through you, you will find that there you turned from light to take something else that was not light. Remain in the light, and Satan can have no power over you, even if a hundred people were to come and stand around you and say to you, "We will join together to bind you, so that you will be crippled," or so that your mind will be affected, or anything. If you know you have the light, you can smile and say, "You can do nothing to me."

Never be afraid of anything. There are two things in the world: one is fear, the other faith. One belongs to the devil; the other to God. If you believe in God, there is no fear. If you sway toward any delusion of Satan, you will be brought into fear. Fear always brings bondage. There is a place of perfect love for Christ in which you are always casting out all fear and you are living in the place of freedom. (See 1 John 4:18.) Be sure that you never allow anything to make you afraid. God is for you; who can be against you (Rom. 8:31)?

The reason why so many people have gone into Christian Science is that the church is barren; it does not have the Holy Spirit. Christian Science exists because the churches have a barren place where the Holy Spirit has not been allowed to rule. There would be no room for Christian Science if the churches were filled with the Holy Spirit. But because the churches had nothing, then the needy people went to the devil to fill the void, and he persuaded them that they had something. Now the same people are coming out knowing they have got nothing—only a wilderness experience.

Let us save ourselves from all this trouble by letting the Holy Spirit fill our hearts.

> Will you be baptized in this faith,
>   Baptized in the Holy Ghost?
> To be free indeed 'tis the power you need,
>   Baptized in the Holy Ghost.

Don't depend on any past tense, any past momentum, but let the anointing be upon you, let the presence and the power be upon you. Are you thirsty, longing, desiring? Then God will pour out of His treasures all you need. God wants to satisfy us with His great, abounding, holy love, imparting love upon love and faith upon faith.

# Preparing for Christ's Return

The cause of all deterioration is refusal of the Holy Spirit. If you have fallen short, it is because you refused the Holy Spirit. Let the Holy Spirit be light in you to lighten even the light that is in you, and no darkness will befall you; you will be kept in the middle of the road.

Look to the coming of the Lord. Set your house in order; be at peace; live at peace; forgive, and learn how to forgive. Never bear malice; don't hold any grudge against anybody. Forgive everybody. It does not matter whether they forgive you or not, you must forgive them. Live in forgiveness; live in repentance; live wholeheartedly. Set your house in order, for God's Son is coming to take what is in the house.

# Two

# The King Is Coming

he life of the Lord Jesus should be so upon us that we are being prepared and made ready for the Rapture. The purpose of this meeting is that the very nature of the Son of God might be presented to us by the Word of Life, so that we may know what this life is. Do we have it? If we do not, can we have it? What will be the evidences of it?

I want you to be so acquainted with the Word of Life that you will have no doubt that you are coming to a similarly precious faith, or that you are coming to the divine life, or that you have a knowledge that One who is greater than you is working out this mighty power of redemption in your mortal bodies.

These are foundation lines. We need to have a foundation of faith before we can begin. God in His omnipotence can bring us into the faith even if we do not have a firm foundation, but I believe that people ought to have things already in line before they begin. The Spirit of the Lord is so mighty that, just as He brought Philip and dropped him down in the desert and brought him back out of the desert (Acts 8:26–40), the same Spirit can come upon the whole church.

35

There is a "knowledge of know," and those who know can speak with confidence about what they do know. I want you to know so that when you go away from here, you will be able to talk about what you know regarding what will happen when Jesus comes, and what will be the cause of the happening—for there has to be a cause of the happening.

### Interpretation of Tongues

Prepare your heart, for the Lord is at the door and waiting now to open your inner vision. For what is created in you is what will come out of you, to be clothed upon with that which is from above. It is not that body, but it is the body that will be.

It is the spiritual body I am dealing with, not the natural body. Let us turn now to the Word of God, the first chapter of John.

### His Life in Us

*"In Him was life, and the life was the light of men"* (John 1:4).

As we go into the Scripture, we will find that this same light, this same spiritual acquaintance or knowledge, this same divine power and authority, the life that is eternal, that is divine and eternal, that is incorruptible, that cannot see corruption—this life was in the Son of God, and He came to be the light and the life of men.

God wants us to comprehend this life that is in the Son, which is meant to be in us, which is to be resurrection, which is to overcome death, which is to have all power in the mortal body. This life is meant to transform the body in every way until it should be in you a manifestation of the invisible but spiritual, the unknown and well known, having nothing and possessing all things. It is to be in you, mightier than you, pulling down strongholds, triumphing graciously over everything.

Now look at the twelfth verse, which has another side to it: *"But as many as received Him..."* (John 1:12). Don't get the idea of receiving the Son of Man in His natural order. If you do, you will miss it. As many as received His life, also received the revelation that was made manifest by Him, the fact that He was in the midst of them with a new order, greater than His natural order, mighty in its production, with forceful language and acts divine, every move supernatural.

*"To them He gave the right to become children of God, to those who believe in His name"* (v. 12). As they received Him, they had power to become acquainted with this inward knowledge of what He was presenting to them. Not His hair, not His head, not His feet, not His hands, not His legs, but the very life that was in Him had to come with power into every living one who understood Him, who received Him.

Now let us look at what power it had to have: *"Who were born, not of blood, nor of the will of the flesh, nor of the will of man, but of God"* (v. 13). Born of God. They know they are confronted with a life and a power that has to come to them, and they are to be absolutely created of it, born of it, made of it. Just as He was, we have to be inwardly, knowing that we are now born of another nature, quickened by another power living in us—a new revelation, having the same things that He had.

He came. Those who believed saw Him. In 1 John we read:

> *That which was from the beginning, which we have heard, which we have seen with our eyes, which we have looked upon, and our hands have handled, concerning the Word of life.*
> (1 John 1:1)

This is not referring to His hands; this is not referring to His eyes. They were looking inward, and they were seeing a new creation; they were seeing a Word with power; they were seeing the nature of God; they were seeing the manifestation of God in human flesh. This is exactly what we are when we are born of this.

*"The life was manifested, and we have seen, and bear witness, and declare to you that eternal life"* (v. 2). Now here is another order, here is another stream. It is not a temporal thing. This is divine, with supernatural power. This is an eternal thing. This is something that cannot pass away. This is something that is to be given to us. This is something that is to be in us. This is the very nature of God. This is as eternal as God. This manifestation of the Son that the disciples were looking at is the Word, the eternal Power, the eternal Source.

### Interpretation of Tongues

It is the Lord. It is the Life from above. It is that which came by the Spirit. He left the throne, He came igniting humanity, until they became a living, quickened spirit of divine order. It is eternal life.

# The King Is Coming

*The life was manifested, and we have seen,
and bear witness, and declare to you that eternal life which was with the Father and was
manifested to us.* (1 John 1:2)

Now they had it, and they began manifesting it
themselves; they began writing about it, and they
knew as they wrote that they were writing Life. The
next verse gives this meaning:

*That which we have seen and heard we declare
to you, that you also may have fellowship with
us; and truly our fellowship is with the Father
and with His Son Jesus Christ.* (v. 3)

First, eternal life comes into you, then your conduct turns heavenward. You begin to fellowship with
the Father, and you become divinely acquainted with
Him, until you know that what was in Him is in you.
This is why they wrote; this is why they knew. And
they expressed it by their mouths, and it became a
quickened, powerful Spirit as they gave it, as it was
when He gave it. I feel the same thing as I am
breathing out this message. I know there is a supernatural, quickening power coming through me by
the Holy Spirit.

## Interpretation of Tongues

Not that which was first; no. God moved
away the first so that He might establish the
second. The first was the natural man, but now
the second is a spiritual man. In you, through
you, by you, coming into manifestation.

Awake! The vision, the life, the power is
now revealed. Enter in, that you might not be
naked when the King comes.

## Smith Wigglesworth on Heaven

God wants to establish in our hearts the fact that we must be ready for the King. Now we are talking about the fact, which is greater than the possibility. Fact works possibilities. Possibilities are in the fact, but you must have the fact first before the possibilities.

### Joy in This Life

To continue with this Scripture in 1 John 1, brought in to show the life manifested, let us consider the fourth verse: *"And these things we write to you that your joy may be full."*

The Word of Life is to make your joy full. We must remember that what is absent in the world is joy. The world has never had joy; the world never will have joy. Joy is not in the five senses of the world. Feelings are there, happiness is there, but joy can only be produced where there is no alloy. Now, there is no alloy in heaven. Alloy means that there is a mixture. In the world there is happiness, but it is a mixture; very often it comes up very close to sorrow. Very often in the midst of festivities there is a place of happiness, and right underneath that there is a very heavy heart and a strange mixture. So, in those five senses that the world has, they have happiness.

But what we have is this: it is joy without alloy, without a mixture. It is inwardly expressive. It rises higher and higher until, if it had its perfect order, we would drown everything with a shout of praise coming from this holy presence.

We want all the people to receive the Holy Spirit because the Holy Spirit has a very blessed expression to the soul or the heart, and it is this: the Holy Spirit has an expression of the Lord in His glory, in His purity, in His power, and in all His blessed words. All these are coming forcefully through as the Holy Spirit is able to witness to you of Him. And every time the Son is manifested in your hearts by the Holy Spirit, you get a real stream of heavenly glory on earth: joy in the Holy Spirit—not in eating and drinking, but in something higher, something better. We all enjoy eating and drinking, but this is something higher, something better, something more substantial: joy in the Holy Spirit! And the Holy Spirit can bring this joy to us.

This is the first foundation of the truths of the coming of the Lord. The coming of the Lord is for the life of the Lord. The coming of the Lord is not for my body. Our bodies will never be in heaven; they will never reach there. They are terrestrial things, and everything terrestrial will finish upon a terrestrial line.

What is going to be there? The Life—the life of the Son of God, the nature of the Son of God, the holiness of the Son of God, the purity. The Life will be there, as well as the likeness and everything pertaining to it.

As we go on, we will see that He is in this life that is going to have a new body. This life will demand a new body; it is demanding it now. We cannot develop this theme in this moment, but I want to throw out some thought of it. This is a law of life. Now, you have a law of life in nature. But now you have to have a law of a spirit of life, which is free from everything of the natural order (Rom. 8:2). And this is the law of life, of the life of Christ that is in you, which I am taking you through or bringing you to, that you may be firmly fixed on the perfect

41

knowledge that no matter what happens, you know you will go.

When I say "you," it is right to say you will go. You will go up, but you, as you now know yourself, won't go in. You will be dissolved as you go. But the nature of the Son, the new life, will go in with your new body.

We move on now to a further foundation. We turn again to the first chapter of John and read the fourteenth verse. They saw, they heard the Word. Now this is to be ours.

> *And the Word became flesh* [they saw it] *and dwelt among us* [it was right in the midst of them, and they couldn't help seeing the glory of it], *and we beheld His glory, the glory as of the only begotten of the Father, full of grace and truth.* (John 1:14)

Now you have to receive that—full of grace, full of truth, the glory of the Lord. You must remember that glory is not a halo around your head. In some paintings of the Lord Jesus or of saints, you will see a light patch painted just over their heads, the idea being to exhibit glory. Glory never is that way. Glory is expressive, and glory is impressive before it is expressive. Glory is not an outside halo; glory is and inward conception.

The more they were in the midst of glory, the more they were convinced of it and preserved it. It had two mighty powers with it: it not only had grace, which was the canopy of the mercy of the high order of God, all the time prevailing and covering and pressing Him, but it also had truth. Christ spoke so that every heart was filled with what He said.

# The King Is Coming

And this is what we have to have. This is what will be caught up and expressed. Can expressiveness be taken up? Yes, because it is the nature of the new birth. Will truth be taken up? Yes, for truth is the very embodiment of the Son. Just as this life permeates through your body, it would be impossible for any saint ever to be free to give anything but absolute truth. The saint has to become an embodiment of truth, life, and Christ manifested. We have to be like Him, just as He was, filled with His glory, this divine order speaking out of fullness, greater than anything we have ever had. Our minds and souls must perceive the things of God so that we live, move, and act in this glory.

They saw it, and you have seen it this morning. The glory of the Lord, the presence of the Lord, the power of the Lord, the life of the Lord is being made manifest. I will tell you how you know it. As I speak, your hearts are burning, your very inward motions are crying out for more. Why? This is what will be taken. It is not you He is after: it is what has been created in you.

## New Life through Christ

How did it come? It wasn't of flesh, it wasn't of blood, it wasn't through the mind of man, but it came by God (John 1:12–13). This new life came by God. You had the other three things before, but then the fourth came. What place did it take? The very thing that would bring you to death changes by beginning in life. The moment this change began in your life, it made you so different, so new, that you felt you had never called God "Father" before in your life; there was something new that said "Father" differently. You knew that you were now joined up to an eternal Fatherhood. You knew you were moved from earth and were joined up to heaven.

The greatest thing that I can talk about this morning is the Rapture, and I touch on it occasionally but cannot go into it yet. The greatest word there is in the world is *rapture*. The worst thing ever that man knows about in the world is death. Death makes you shudder. There is something about it that makes nobody want it. But this new life frees you from death. You know there is no death in it. It is life. This eternal life, this inward force, makes you know as you think about rapture that you are not here, you are far off. That is why I want to get you into thinking that you are far off, and I want you to live in a place of divine acquaintance with the Rapture. You have to get to know how to possess your souls in patience (Luke 21:19).

Now look at the third chapter of John:

*Jesus answered, "Most assuredly, I say to you, unless one is born of water and the Spirit, he cannot enter the kingdom of God. That which is born of the flesh is flesh, and that which is born of the Spirit is spirit. Do not marvel that I said to you, 'You must be born again.' The wind blows where it wishes, and you hear the sound of it, but cannot tell where it comes from and where it goes. So is everyone who is born of the Spirit." Nicodemus answered and said to Him, "How can these things be?"* (John 3:5–9)

So we see that no natural man who ever lived can understand these things. This is a supernatural teaching, and when we come to the line of this truth, we are able to put supernatural things into place to discern natural things. But we must be supernatural first, before we can deal with supernatural things. (See 1 Corinthians 2:14.)

Jesus was a supernatural evidence, and He was dealing with a supernatural process. Here, He was dealing with a man who was natural. This man who was natural could not comprehend how it could be possible for him, who had been born, say, forty-five or fifty years before, to be born again.

## The New Birth

Jesus spoke to Nicodemus as I am speaking to you this morning, and He told him that this birth, this new birth, is not flesh and blood; this new birth is the life of God. It is a spiritual life, as real as God, as true as God, and as forming as God. God is a formation, and we are formed after His formation, for He made us in His very image. But He is a spiritual God, and He has quickened us and made us to be like Him with an inward, spiritual life. Just as we have natural formation, so the new nature, the new power, is continually forming a new man in us after the order of Him. The first Adam was formed, and we are in the vision of him; the last Adam, the new creation, is going to have a vision and expression like Him. As we have borne the image of the earthly, we are going to bear the image of the heavenly (1 Cor. 15:49).

It is already in us, but the vessel is not broken. The container will be dissolved, and the heavenly nature, the heavenly body, will prove itself, and we will be like Him.

I want you to follow the word and rightly discern its meaning, asking yourself these questions: Am I in the faith? Do I have what Nicodemus was seeking?

I was once exactly where Nicodemus was, and said, *"How can these things be?"* (John 3:9). Then there came by faith a regenerating power that made me know I was born of God. It came like the wind. I could not see it, but I felt it. It had a tremendous effect upon my human nature, and I found that I myself was a new creation. I found I wanted to pray and to talk about the Lord. Oh, I will never forget saying "Father."

If you catch this truth, it does not matter where you are. If you are in exile somewhere—on a farm where no one is near you, exiled from everybody, and cannot get near anybody for comfort—if this life gets into you, you will know that when He comes again, you will go to meet Him.

This is the life that I want you to know, the life in the body. The new birth, the new creation, the quickening, the being made after Him, being begotten of God—these are very beautiful thoughts if you put them in this perfect order. When you are born of God, God's nature comes in. I won't call it the germ of eternal life, but the seed of God, because we are conceived by the Word, we are quickened by the power, we are made after His order. What is from above has entered into what is below, and you have now become a quickened spirit. You were dead, without aspiration, and without desire. As soon as this comes in, aspiration, desire, and prayer ascend, lifting higher and higher, and you have already moved toward heavenly things.

# The King Is Coming

This is a new creation that cannot live on the earth. It always lives, soaring higher—higher and higher, loftier and loftier, holier and holier. This is the most divine order you could have. This is the spiritual order, God manifested in the flesh, quickening us by the Spirit, making us like Him. Hallelujah!

## Know and Believe

Now turn to the gospel of John:

> *Most assuredly, I say to you, he who hears My word and believes in Him who sent Me has everlasting life, and shall not come into judgment, but has passed from death into life.*
>
> (John 5:24)

*"He who hears."* Does this mean that the Word of Life can go into the ear? Yes, in through the ear, right into the heart—the word, the life, the nature of the Son of God.

What does it do? *"He who hears My word and believes in Him who sent Me has everlasting life."* Who can put limits on that?

There is a good deal of controversy about the length of time this life lasts. How long do you say it lasts? What does Jesus say it is? *"Everlasting life."* Some people say it might be for ten, fifteen, or twenty years. What do you say it is? *"Everlasting life."*

If you get there, there is no difficulty about being ready. But if you doubt the Word of God, how can you be ready? I am speaking to the wise, and a word to the wise is sufficient. It does not matter who brings a quarrelsome accusation against the Word. If he says anything about this everlasting life, ask him

47

what he believes about it, for Jesus said this: *"He who hears My word and believes in Him who sent Me has everlasting life."*

Suppose you say, "Well, I doubt it." Then you will be done. Jesus said that if you doubt it, it is damnation; if you believe it, it is everlasting life. It just depends upon what you are going to believe about it. Do you believe it is everlasting life? Are you going to let your opinions rob you and bring you into condemnation? Or are you going to receive what the Word says?

What is the Word? The Word is truth. What is truth? Jesus is truth. Jesus said these words: *"He who hears My word and believes in Him who sent Me has everlasting life, and shall not come into judgment, but has passed from death into life."*

Holy, holy, holy, Lord God of Hosts!
Heaven and earth are praising Thee,
O Lord, Most High!

These meetings will go higher and higher. I want you to get a foundation position, so that when you go out in the world of service, you will have laid down a fact in your heart as to what is the coming of the Lord. As I go on, I will be able to give you a clear distinction of its expression—a living expression of a living personality. Christ is now already manifested or being manifested in us. The sons of God are coming forth with power, and God will show us, as we go on with the Word of God, this living glorious fact, or hope, or crown of rejoicing.

May God the Holy Spirit sanctify us and purify us with a perfect purification, until we stand white in the presence of God. Let us do some repenting; let us tell God we want to be holy. If you are sure you have this eternal life in you, I want you to consider it worthy not to look back, keeping your eyes upon the plan, looking toward the Master. Believe that God is greater than your heart. Believe that God is greater than your thoughts. Believe that God is greater than the devil. Believe that He will preserve you. Believe in His almightiness. And on the authority of God's faith in you, you will triumph until He comes.

> Bring me higher up the mountain,
> Into fellowship with Thee!
> In Thy light I see the Fountain,
> And the Blood that cleanseth me.

## Questions Answered

**Q:** You said there is no body in heaven. Is Jesus Christ sitting at the right hand of the Father in flesh or in spirit?

**A:** We will have bodies in heaven, but they will be spiritual, glorified bodies. I believe that Jesus is different from anyone else in the glory because of the marks of the Crucifixion. But I have Scripture to bear me out that there is no flesh and blood in heaven, but we will be different. We will have our hands, but they will be glorified hands, on glorified bodies. Your own character, your own crown, will be there.

How will the crown be made? The crown is this: the wood, the hay, the stubble will be burned, and the gold, the silver, and precious stones will be left. Everybody will know what kind of a crown or life they have had because the crown will be made up of their own gold and their own precious stones after they have gone through the fire.

Everybody will know. We will know as we are known; there will be no mistake about that. But it will be an expression of brightness, of glory. For instance, we will be really transparent in so many ways; the glory will be so wonderful.

Let us look at Jesus for a moment. When Jesus was with Peter and John on that holy mount, the very vesture, the very nature, everything that He had was turned to transparent glory until even His clothing was as white as snow and the whole of His body was transformed in that vision. (See Matthew 17:1–8.)

The very thing that was in each person on earth will be exactly expressed in heaven. Moses and Elijah were known in their glorified bodies. Jesus will be known to everybody as the Son of God and as the Lamb that was slain. The marks will be there, the glorified body with the marks of the cross. It will be very wonderful. We will be there. What will have passed away from us is this: the marks of sin, the marks of deformity, the marks of corruption, the marks of transgression. We will be there, whiter than snow, purified through and through.

The Lamb of God will be known; He will be different, He will have a glorified body, for flesh and blood do not enter into the kingdom of God. They could not stand the glory; they would be withered up in His presence; so the body has to be a changed body. God calls it in 1 Corinthians 15 the *"celestial"* body (v. 40).

# The King Is Coming

**Q:** Didn't Christ after the Resurrection have a body of flesh and bones?
**A:** Yes, He did. When we get to heaven, what we will be most pleased about at first is that He will be the same Lord, just the same, only in a glorified body. He will be neither flesh nor bones.

**Q:** What did Job mean when he said, *"After my skin is destroyed, this I know, that in my flesh I shall see God"* (Job 19:26)?
**A:** That is a different thing altogether. I believe that everybody will see God perfectly and in a very wonderful way. The pure in heart will see God (Matt. 5:8). I believe we will see God and see Jesus in our flesh, but it will be the last time of the flesh; we will know Him no more after the flesh, but we will see Him in the spirit. You will never see Jesus anymore after that in the flesh.

**Q:** Will the celestial bodies and terrestrial bodies be gathered together?
**A:** Terrestrial bodies will never be in the presence of God. Terrestrial is always earthly. Celestial bodies in the glory will leave terrestrial bodies, and we will all be together—the angels, archangels, God— all will be there, perfect. The angels may never understand the fullness of our redemption, but they will all be there in perfect harmony. God will gather all into perfect harmony. Heaven will be a wonderful, glorious place. However, in order to prepare us properly, He knows it will be necessary to have a new earth and a new heaven to fit the situation.

**Q:** Is there a Scripture that says that the Christians of today without the baptism of the Holy Spirit go up in the Rapture?

**A:** What is the Rapture but eternal life? Could you imagine that anything down here that has had eternal life within would not be in the Rapture? It is contrary to the mind of God, contrary to the teaching of God. It is impossible for anyone to have eternal life in them and not also have that life that will lead to heaven; for eternal life, the life within you, is the life and the nature of the Son, and when He comes it is impossible for you not to go with Him. *"When Christ who is our life appears, then you also will appear with Him in glory"* (Col. 3:4). What will make it? The life, the joint life.

**Q:** Will we see the Father as a personality, or will Jesus be the expression of the Father?

**A:** One thing will be certain: when we get to glory, we will be very much taken up with the Son, but we must not forget that the Son will not rob the Father of His glory. Rather, He will take us all, and He will take Himself in the great Day of all things, and He will present us all and Himself to the Father. So I know the Father will be in a glorious place in glory; and I know the Son will be in a wonderful place; and I know the Holy Spirit who has comforted us all— what a great joy it will be to see Him who has been the great Comforter and the great Leader and the great Speaker and the great Operator. We will surely give Him a great place in glory!

**Q:** Is it possible after a person has been truly born again to get away from the Lord and to be lost?

# The King Is Coming

**A:** The Scripture says, *"He who believes in [the Lord] has everlasting life"* (John 6:47). The Word of God will not change for anyone. The Word of God is like a two-edged sword, dividing even the soul and the spirit (Heb. 4:12), and it is all the time putting away what man says and giving you what God says.

**Q:** You said if our eyes are open we could see the Lord right among us. We know that He ascended in one body. How could that be, provided there were half a dozen meetings going on at the same time— how could He be right in the midst?

**A:** The Holy Spirit is here and—I want to say it reverently—Jesus is not here. Don't misunderstand me. Has Jesus ever been here since He went to the glory? No. Is He coming to the earth the next time? No; He is coming in the heavens, and we will meet Him.

But what is here? The Holy Spirit, and He makes Jesus just as real to me as if He were here. That is the position of the Holy Spirit—to reveal the Father and the Son—and He makes them just as real to us as if they were here. The Holy Spirit fills the whole earth, and He could make a million assemblies see every spiritual thing possible. We do not want to see spirits; we want to see bodies filled with the Spirit of the living God.

For our comfort and consolation, He says, *"Lo, I am with you always"* (Matt. 28:20), and He is with us in power and in might. The Holy Spirit makes Him real to me. He is with me.

**Q:** *"Most assuredly, I say to you, he who believes in Me has everlasting life"* (John 6:47). Does not this verse hinge on the word *"believes"*? That is a present, continuous tense. He believes now, and he keeps right at it. Do gaining the glory and keeping the eternal life not depend on whether or not we keep believing? First John says, *"If our heart does not condemn us, we have confidence"* (1 John 3:21), and then we can believe. If I do something that makes my heart condemn me, how can I keep on believing?

**A:** If eternal life in you depends upon your always thinking about nothing else but eternal life, most of the people in this place would say, "Well, I am no good then." But we must remember that the blood of Jesus is not a past-tense cleansing power, but it is a present-tense cleansing power. When you are asleep at night, you know very well you neither try to believe nor think about believing anything. Even so, the blood of Jesus cleanses you in the night, and He cleanses you right now. Your salvation does not consist of your always shouting, "I believe!"

The new birth is a new life; it is regenerative, it is holy, it is divine, it is faith, it is Christ. He is with you always, moving you, changing you, thrilling you, causing you to live in the glory without pressure. It is a believing position. *"I delight to do Your will"* (Ps. 40:8). My condition of salvation is not something that pressures me continually to say I believe or else I will be lost. Faith is a life; life is a presence, a presence of changing from one state of glory to another.

My attitude of yieldedness to God continually keeps me in His favor. If I thought that my salvation depended upon that, I would know then that I had lost the knowledge that God was greater than my heart and greater than my life, for I am not kept by what I do, but I am kept by the power of God.

**Q:** Doesn't His keeping power depend on my doing the same things as I did when I gained His favor?
**A:** What you are doing is putting your weakness in the place of God's almighty power. If you believe, you are kept from falling. After God gives faith, He does not take it away.

**Q:** I know a number of people who have truly belonged to God, and the glory has been upon them, but today they are serving the devil just as faithfully as they ever served the Lord. They have lost eternal life, have they not?
**A:** You are not responsible for them. They have had the light. Light has come to the world, and they refused light. They are in awful jeopardy and darkness and sorrow. If you do not allow God to be greater than your heart, you will be in trouble about them.

**Q:** I am not in trouble about them, but I cannot quite catch the thought that they are still saved.
**A:** I have not told you that they are still saved. I believe they have tasted, but they have never been converted. I tell you the reason why: Jesus said, *"My sheep...follow Me"* (John 10:27), and they are not of the fold if they do not follow. Jesus said it.

If I find people who want me to believe that they belong to God, and they are following the devil, I will say, "Well, either you or the Word is a liar." I do not take it for granted that because a person says he has been saved that he is saved. He is only proving to me he is saved if he follows.

# Smith Wigglesworth on Heaven

Don't you for a moment believe I am here standing for eternal security. I am trying to help you to see that God's eternal security can be so manifested in your mortal bodies that there could not be a doubt about rapture or life or anything. I want the Word of God to make you know that it is the eternal Word; it is the eternal life, and it is eternal power.

I have never known a moment in my life in which God has not made me long for more holiness. I have been saved for sixty years, and I have never lost the sense of that saving, peaceful place. *"He who believes in the Son of God has the witness"* (1 John 5:10). I cannot change the Word of God because a few people tasted and then went away. I believe that when you have really been born of God, you are either in deep conviction or you are on the top. It could not be otherwise.

**Q:** Will you please explain Ezekiel 18:24, which says, *"But when a righteous man turns away from his righteousness and commits iniquity, and does according to all the abominations that the wicked man does, shall he live?"*
**A:** We ought to see that our righteousness is greater than the righteousness of filthy rags. We ought to see that our holiness is so purified that we are not holy for the sake of being holy, but we are holy because of an incarnation of God in us making us holy.

It is necessary that we face the truth and get to know it. If we do not, what an awful awaiting will be ours! The books are not to be opened and the crown is not to be given until the end. But I know some crowns are being increased, and I know God is making a great preparation for the saints.

# The King Is Coming

But I warn you today: see to it that your lives are holy; see to it that you do not give place to the devil; see to it that you buy opportunities; see to it that your whole body is sanctified and made ready for God, as the Scripture says. See to it that no sin ever has anything to do with your life. Believe God that He can keep you from falling. Believe God that He can present you holy. Believe God that you can have a reward. I am going in for the reward. Because other people do not care for going in for the reward, it makes me all the more earnest for it.

Three

# Life Everlasting

ou may be amazed, when you step into the heavenly glory, to find there the very Word, the very life, the very touch that has caused aspiration and inspiration. The Word is settled there. The Word creates right in our very nature this wonderful touch of divine inspiration, making us know that those who are in heaven and we who are on earth are of one spirit, blended in one harmonious knowledge, created in a new order. We are being made like Him by the power of the spirit of the Word of God, until we are full of hopefulness, filled with life, joyously expecting, gloriously waiting.

One word is continually sufficient for me:

> *Therefore, having been justified by faith, we have peace with God through our Lord Jesus Christ, through whom also we have access by faith into this grace in which we stand, and rejoice in hope of the glory of God.* (Rom. 5:1–2)

Salvation fills us with the *"hope of the glory of God,"* with a great access into the grace.

# Smith Wigglesworth on Heaven

Let us turn to the sixth chapter of John. We are still on the foundation of the construction of the saint of God in the new order of the Spirit. We are still building upon the foundation principles of the living Word of God, not so that we may be like those who are drunk in the night, or those who are asleep, but so that we will be awakened. (See 1 Thessalonians 5:5–8.)

Being awakened does not mean particularly that you have been actually asleep; the word *sleeping* in this context doesn't mean a person is actually asleep. It means that he is dense to activity relating to the spiritual realm. Sleeping does not mean that you are fast asleep. Sleeping means that you have lost understanding, you are dull of hearing, and your eyes are heavy because they are not full of the light that will light you. So God is causing us to understand that we have to be alive and awake.

Here is the word: *"Do not labor for the food which perishes"* (John 6:27). At the beginning of John 6, Jesus had been feeding the sheep, and because they were being fed by His gracious hands, the crowd came around Him again. He saw that they were of the natural order, and He broke forth into this wonderful word, *"Do not labor for the food which perishes."*

## Interpretation of Tongues

The Lord Jesus, seeing the needy missing the great ideal of His mission, turned their attention by saying, "It is more needful that you get a drink of a spiritual awakening. It is more needful that you eat of the inner manna of Christ today, for God has sealed Him for that purpose and He has become the Bread for you."

# Life Everlasting

The Master was in earnest when He said, *"Enter by the narrow gate; for wide is the gate and broad is the way that leads to destruction"* (Matt. 7:13).

Strive to enter in at the narrow gate. Get a live, inward inheritance in you. See that the Master has food for us, bread enough and to spare.

## Interpretation of Tongues

It is the living Word. It is the touch of His own spiritual nature that He wants to breathe into our human nature today.

It is the nature of the Son; it is the breath of His life; it is the quickening of His power; it is the savor of life unto life. It is that which quickens you from death into life; it is that which wakens you out of all human into the glorious liberty of the sons of God. It is the Spirit that quickens.

Let me read the Word:

*Do not labor for the food which perishes, but for the food which endures to everlasting life, which the Son of Man will give you, because God the Father has set His seal on Him.*
                                        (John 6:27)

Everlasting life is a gift. The Holy Spirit is a gift. But *"the gift of God is eternal life"* (Rom. 6:23), and we have this life in His Son (1 John 5:11). *"He who does not have the Son of God does not have life"* (v. 12), but he who has the Son *"has passed from death into life"* (John 5:24). This is the life that will be caught up; this is the life that will be changed in a moment; this is the life that will enter into the presence of

God in a moment of time, because it is divine, because it has no bondage, because it is not hindered by the flesh.

## The Beginning of Life

So God is pruning us, teaching us to observe that those who enter into this life have ceased from their own works (Heb. 4:10). Those who enter into this spiritual awakening have no more bondages. They have learned that *"no one engaged in warfare entangles himself with the affairs of this life"* (2 Tim. 2:4). They have a new inspiration of divine power. It is the nature of the Son of God.

But the verse says, *"Strive to enter through the narrow gate"* (Luke 13:24). Yes, beloved, this means you will have to work for it, because your own nature will interfere with you; your friends will often stand in the way. Your position will many times almost bring you to a place where you will be doomed if you take that stand.

I understand that Jesus could be interpreted in no other way but this: *"Whoever desires to save his life will lose it, but whoever loses his life for My sake will find it"* (Matt. 16:25). He will find the life that never ceases. Human life has an end; divine life has only a beginning. This is the life that the Son of Man was sealed to give. He was specially sealed; He was specially anointed; He was specially separated. He gave Himself over to God, so that He might become the firstfruit of the first-begotten of a new creation that was going to be in the presence of God forever. A new creation, a new sonship, a new adoption, a new place, a new power. Hallelujah! Are you in for it?

# Life Everlasting

The apostle Peter had entered into this divine position just before Jesus made His statement, *"Whoever desires to save his life will lose it, but whoever loses his life for My sake will find it"* (Matt. 16:25). Peter had just gotten this new life; he had just entered into the place where he knew that Jesus was the Son of God, saying, *"You are the Christ, the Son of the living God"* (v. 16). Then Jesus began breaking the seal of His ministry. He said, *"The Son of Man must be delivered into the hands of sinful men, and be crucified, and the third day rise again"* (Luke 24:7).

Peter said, "This will not happen. I'll see to that! You leave that business with me. Let anybody touch you, and I will stand in your place; I will be with you." And Jesus said, *"Get behind Me, Satan! You are an offense to Me, for you are not mindful of the things of God, but the things of men"* (Matt. 16:23).

Anything that hinders me from falling into the ground, everything that interferes with my taking up my cross, dying to self, separating from the world, cleaning my life up, or entering through the narrow gate, anything that interferes with that is Satan's power. *"Unless a grain of wheat falls into the ground and dies, it remains alone"* (John 12:24).

Strive to enter in. Seek to be worthy to enter in. Let God be honored by your leaving behind the things that you know are taking your life, hindering your progress, blighting your prospects, and ruining your mind—for nothing will dull the mind's perceptions like touching earthly things that are not clean.

When God began dealing with me on holy lines, I was working for thirteen saloons, meaning that I was going to thirteen different bars. Of course, I was

among hundreds of other customers. God dealt with me in this matter, and I cleared up the whole situation in the presence of God. That was only one thing; there were a thousand things.

God wants us to be holy, pure, and perfect the whole way through. The inheritance is an incorruptible inheritance; it is undefiled, and it does not fade away (1 Pet. 1:4). Those who are entering in are judging themselves so that they will not be condemned with the world (1 Cor. 11:32). Many people have fallen asleep. (See verses 27–30.) Why? Because they did not listen to the correction of the Word of the Lord. Some have been ill, and God dealt with them; they would not heed, and then God put them to sleep.

Oh, that God the Holy Spirit will have a choice with us today, that we will judge ourselves so that we are not condemned with the world! *"For if we would judge ourselves, we would not be judged"* (v. 31). What is it to judge yourself? If the Lord speaks, if He says, "Let it go," no matter if it is as dear as your right eye, you must let it go. If it is as costly as your right foot, you must let it go. It is far better to let it go.

Strive to enter in.

### Interpretation of Tongues

God's Word never speaks in vain. It always opens to you the avenues where you can enter in. God opens the door for you. He speaks to your heart; He is dealing with you. We are dealing with the coming of the Lord, but how will we be prepared unless all is burned? The wood, the hay, the stubble must be burned. The gold, the silver, and the precious stones will be preserved.

# Life Everlasting

Be willing, beloved, for the Lord Himself has to deal with you.

## The Bread of Life

Let us move on to another important lesson of Scripture:

*Then Jesus said to them, "Most assuredly, I say to you, Moses did not give you the bread from heaven, but My Father gives you the true bread from heaven. For the bread of God is He who comes down from heaven and gives life to the world."* (John 6:32–33)

Bread! Oh, beloved, I want God to give you a spiritual appetite so that you will have a great inward devouring place where you will eat the Word, where you will savor it with joy, where you will have it with grace, and also where it will be mingled with separation. As the Word comes to you—the Word of God, the Bread of Heaven, the very thing you need, the very nature of the life of the Son of God—and as you eat, you will be made in a new order after Him who has created you for His plan and purpose.

*"Then they said to Him, 'Lord, give us this bread always'"* (v. 34). I want that same expression to be made in our hearts because He is helping us into this.

*"And Jesus said to them, 'I am the bread of life. He who comes to Me shall never hunger, and he who believes in Me shall never thirst'"* (John 6:35).

The process of the Word of God must kindle in us a separation from the world. It must bring death to everything except the life of the Word of Christ in our hearts. I want to save you from judging, because to the degree that you have not come into the revelation of this eternal working in you, to that degree you will not come right through believing in the true principle of the Word of Life.

*"He who comes to Me shall never hunger, and he who believes in Me shall never thirst."*

The two things are necessary. I will never expect any person to go beyond his light. The Word of God is to give you light. The Spirit of the Lord and the Word of the Lord—one is light, the other is life. We must see that God wants us to have these two divine properties, life and light, so that we are in a perfect place to judge ourselves by the Word of God. The Word of God will stand true, whatever our opinions may be. Scripture says very truly, *"For what if some did not believe? Will their unbelief make the faithfulness of God without effect?"* (Rom. 3:3). Will it change the Word? The Word of God will be the same whether people believe it or not.

In these meetings, God will sift the believer. This is a sifting meeting. I want you to get away from the chaff. Chaff is judgment; chaff is unbelief; chaff is fear; chaff is failing. It is the covering of the weak, and as long as it covers the weak, it hinders the weak from coming forth for bread. So God has to deal with the chaff; He has to get it away so that you might be the pure bread, the pure life, the pure word, and so that there will be no strange thing in you, no misunderstanding.

God has to deal with His people, and if God deals with the house of God, then the world will soon be dealt with. The dealing first is with the house of God, and then after that with the world (1 Pet. 4:17). When the house of God is right, all the people will get right very soon. The principle is this: all the world needs and longs to be right, and so we have to be salt and light to guide them, to lead them, to operate before them so that they see our good works and glorify our Lord.

I was preaching on these divine elements one day, and one person in the midst of the meeting said, "I won't believe! I won't believe! Nothing like that ever moves me. You cannot move me. Nothing can move me."

"I believe! I believe! I believe!" I responded.

I went on dealing with the things of God. This man was a well-known preacher. He had come to a place where the chaff had to be taken up, where God was dealing with him, where his life was opened out. He said again, "I won't believe!" It made no difference to me; I went on preaching. He was so aroused that he jumped up and went out, shouting as he closed the door, "I won't believe!"

The next morning, the pastor of the church at which the meeting was being held, got a note saying, "Please come immediately," and the pastor went. As soon as he got to the door, a woman met him, tears in her eyes, weeping bitterly.

"Oh," she said, "I am in great distress!"

She took him inside. When he got inside, the first thing that confronted him was the man who had shouted out, "I won't believe!" The man got a piece of paper and wrote, "Last night I had a chance to believe; I refused to believe, and now I cannot believe, and I cannot speak."

This man was made mute because he would not believe. Is he the only one? No. We read the story of Zacharias and Elizabeth. When Zacharias was in the

Holy of Holies, God spoke to him, telling him that He was going to give him a son. But his heart was unmoved, and his language was contrary to faith; so Gabriel said to him, *"You will be mute and not able to speak...because you did not believe"* (Luke 1:20). And he came out of that place mute.

It seems to me that if we will not judge ourselves, we will be judged (1 Cor. 11:31). I am giving you the Word. The Word should so be in you that, as I speak, the fire should burn, the life should be kindled, the very nature of Christ should transform you. You should be so moved in this meeting that you are ready for rapture, and longing for it. You know that you have the life, and you know this life will be held until it gets loose.

You need the Bread to feed the life to you. The Word of God is the Bread. There is no famine going on now; God is giving us the Bread of Life.

*"He who comes to Me shall never hunger, and he who believes in Me shall never thirst"* (John 6:35). It is a constant satisfaction, an inward joyful expression, a place of peace.

> *All that the Father gives Me will come to Me, and the one who comes to Me I will by no means cast out. For I have come down from heaven, not to do My own will, but the will of Him who sent Me. This is the will of the Father who sent Me, that of all He has given Me I should lose nothing, but should raise it up at the last day.* (vv. 37–39)

Nothing—I will lose nothing! Do you believe that? Some people are still on the hedge, undecided.

# Life Everlasting

"After all, He may lose us." I would rather believe the Word of God!

## Only Believe

I find people continually deceived because they look around them, and many people have lost all because of their feelings. There was one man in the Old Testament who was very terribly deceived because of his feelings—it was Jacob. He felt for Esau, but he was deceived. If you feel, you will be deceived.

God does not want us to feel. He wants us on one line only: believing. I would like you to understand that you did not come to Jesus. God gave you to Jesus. Where did He find you? He found you in the world, and He gave you to Jesus, and Jesus gave you eternal life. As He received everyone whom He had given His life for and given His life to, He said He would lose nothing; He would preserve them.

"Oh," you say, "that all depends."

Yes, it does, it depends upon whether you believe God or not. But I find people always getting outside of the plan of God because they use their own judgment.

I am not going to believe that all who say they are believers, believe. There was one group who came up to Jesus and said, "We are the seed of Abraham; we have Abraham for our father." (See John 8:39.) He said, "You are mistaken; you are the seed of the devil." (See verses 39–44.)

*"He who believes in the Son of God has the witness"* (1 John 5:10), and we know that we are the sons of God because we do those things that please Him. We know we are the sons of God because we

69

love to keep His commandments. *"His command-ments are not grievous"* (1 John 5:3 KJV). And we know we are the sons of God because we overcome the world. (See verse 4.)

That is what every son of God has to do—overcome the world. And this life we receive from Him is eternal and everlasting and cannot see corruption. But God is feeding us this morning with that wonderful Word of promise, so that we might know that we have the inheritance in the Spirit, and so that we may know that we are going on to the place of "Ready, Lord, ready!"

Are you ready to go? I am here getting you ready to go, because you have to go. It is impossible for the life of God or the law of the life of the Spirit to be in you unless it is doing its work. The law of the life of the Spirit will be putting to death all the natural life and will quicken you continually with spiritual life until you will have to go.

When I see white hair and wrinkled faces, I say, "You have to go. It does not matter what you say, you cannot stop; you have to go. You will begin blossoming, and in a short time you will bloom and be off."

That is a natural plan, but I am talking about a supernatural plan. We know that as we have borne the image of the earthly, we are going to bear the image of the heavenly (1 Cor. 15:49). Mortality will be swallowed up in life. The very nature of the Son of God is in us, making life, immortality, and power. The power of the Word of the living Christ!

The Gospel of the grace of God has power to bring immortality and life. What is the Gospel? The Word, the Bread of the Son of God. Feed upon it.

# Life Everlasting

Feed upon it in your heart. It is immortality; it is life by the Word of quickening and by the Word of truth.

You look good, you are an inspiration, but you know there are many marks and blemishes. You know that as you pass through the weary days of toil, battling with sin on every line, there is a light in you, a life in you that is going to pass off, and you are going to be like Him. It will be the same face, but the marks, the scars, and the spots will have gone. What will do it? The Bread! Oh, Lord, ever more give us this Bread, the Bread of the Son of God!

*"Most assuredly, I say to you, he who believes in Me has everlasting life. I am the bread of life"* (John 6:47–48). Everlasting life means Bread. Men cannot live by bread alone, but by the Word of the living God (Matt. 4:4).

## Tried by Fire, Enriched by Grace

When I read this in the book of Revelation, my heart was moved: *"And His name is called The Word of God"* (Rev. 19:13). His name, the very name, is the Word of God, who gave His life for the world. And of His life, of His Spirit, of His grace, of His faith we have received. What does this mean? Oh, you tried ones, grace is being poured into you—grace from heaven, grace enriched, grace abundant. His grace is for your weakness, so that you might be sustained in the trial, in the fire, passing through it, coming out more like the Lord.

This inspires me. Why? Because time comes to an end. All the beautiful buildings in the world, the mountains, the heavens and all, will pass away. The heavens will be rolled up as a scroll (Isa. 34:4), and all things *"will melt with fervent heat"* (2 Pet. 3:10). But one thing cannot be burned; one thing cannot be changed; one thing can stand the fire, the water, persecution, and anything else. What is it? The same thing that went into the fire and remained untouched while the men on the outside were slain by the fire.

Shadrach, Meshach, and Abednego were in the fire, and it did not burn them. The king was amazed when he saw them walking. "Oh!" he said. *"Did we not cast three men bound into the midst of the fire?"* (Dan. 3:24).

*"True, O king"* (v. 24), his men replied.

*"'Look!' he answered, 'I see four men loose, walking in the midst of the fire...and the form of the fourth is like the Son of God'"* (v. 25).

There is no consuming. There is a life of the Son of God that cannot be burned, cannot see corruption, passes through fire, passes through clouds, passes through legions of demons and will clear them out of the way, passes through everything. Oh, that life! What is it? The life of the Son of God. He came to give life; He came to give life more abundantly. Oh, what a life, abounding life, resurrection life!

Do you have it? Is it yours? Are you afraid you will lose it? Do you believe He will lose you?

"What makes you say that?" you ask.

Because sometimes I hear doubters. So I am going to read a wonderful Scripture for the doubters.

> *My sheep hear My voice, and I know them, and they follow Me. And I give them eternal life, and they shall never perish; neither shall anyone snatch them out of My hand. My Father, who has given them to Me, is greater than all;*

# Life Everlasting

*and no one is able to snatch them out of My Father's hand.*　　　　(John 10:27–29)

Oh, that life—full of deity, full of assurance, full of victory, full of a shout. There is the shout of a King in the midst of you this morning. Will you be ready? How can you help it? Is it possible not to be ready? Why, it is not your life, it is His life. You did not seek Him; it was He who sought you. You cannot keep yourself; it is He who keeps you. You did not make the offering; it was God who made the offering. So it is all of grace. But what a wonderful grace!

## Interpretation of Tongues

The trumpet will blow and all will be brought forth, for God will bring them with Him, and those who are awake will not interfere with those who are asleep, but all with one breath will rise. What will rise? The life will rise to meet the Life that has preserved it, and we will be ever with the Lord.

What is going? The life. He gives everlasting life, and they will never perish.

Oh, where is your faith? Is your faith inspired? Are you quickened? Is there within you a truth that is saying, "I feel it, I know it. It moves me; I have it"? Yes, and you will be there in heaven—as surely as you are here, you will be there.

This thing that we are entering into is going to continue forever. Let us feed on this Bread; let us live in this holy atmosphere. This is divine nature that God is causing us to know, which will last forever.

Keep us, Lord, in a place of buying up opportunities, burning up bridges, paying the prices, denying ourselves so that we might be worthy of being Your own forever.

## Questions Answered

**Q:** Is there distinction in the Word between the life that brings forth the Rapture and eternal life where some first go down into the grave?

**A:** No. Those asleep in Jesus have the same life, but they are not asleep in the grave. They fall asleep to rest, but it is not a sleep or a rest of the spirit. The spirit never sleeps; the soul never sleeps. Solomon wrote, *"I sleep, but my heart is awake"* (Song 5:2). Remember that the moment the body is put to rest, the spirit requires no rest; it is always young, it will know nothing about time.

Whichever way the body goes, it will be the same. If it goes to the grave, what will happen? The body, all that is earthly, will pass away; it will come to dust. Suppose it goes up. The Word of God says it will be dissolved. The same thing, it will be dissolved either way it goes. Why? Because flesh and blood are not going there, but the life of the Son of God is. God will provide a new body, resembling the old in every way—likeness, character, everything. The human spirit will enter into a celestial body whether it goes up or down—only we want you all to go up.

**Q:** I have heard Revelation 3:5 brought up to prove that a name could be blotted out of the Book of Life. Will you please explain?

# Life Everlasting

**A:** I am dealing with people who are receiving everlasting life, who are not going to be lost. I am persuaded of better things than that of you. I will never believe that any human being is greater than my God. I believe that God is greater than all and that God can preserve us all. But I do believe that there are any number of people who have tried to make people believe they are the seed of God when they have not really been born again.

The life of the new birth is always seeking after God; it has no time for falling away from God, no time for the world; it is always hungry for God. Unless you get this fundamental truth deep down in your heart, you will fail, because you have to go on to holiness, inseparableness. *"Holiness adorns Your house, O LORD"* (Ps. 93:5). How can you be anything but holy and long to be holy?

Four

# The Abiding Spirit

od seems to fascinate me with His Word. I read and read, and yet it is all something so new, remarkable, and blessed. I realize the truth of that saying, "The bride rejoices to hear the Bridegroom's voice." (See John 3:29.) The Word is His voice, and as we get nearer to Jesus, we understand that He came to take out for Himself a people that should be His bride. It is not only to be saved, my brother, but there is an eternal destiny awaiting us of all the wonderment that God has in the glory. I pray that we may see that God in His mercy has given us this blessed revelation of how He lived, loved, and had power to say to those disciples, "Some of you shall not see death until you see the kingdom of God coming in power." (See Mark 9:1.)

Oh, that blessed Christ, who could pray until His countenance was changed and became so glorious, until His raiment became white and glistening. He said, "I have power to lay down My life, and I have power to take it again." (See John 10:17.) It is true that by wicked hands He was taken and crucified, but He had to be willing, for He had all power and could have called on legions of angels to help Him and deliver Him from death. But oh, that blessed Christ had purposed to save us and bring us into fellowship and oneness with Himself. He went right through death so that He might impart unto us the blessed reconciliation between God and man.

So it is that the Man Jesus Christ, who is the Atonement for the whole world, who is the Son of God, is also the sinner's Friend. *"He was wounded for our transgressions"* (Isa. 53:5). This blessed Christ gave His disciples the glory that He had with the Father before the world was. (See John 17:5.) Oh, it is lovely, and I believe that God wants us to know that He will withhold *"no good thing...from those who walk uprightly"* (Ps. 84:11), including health, peace, joy in the Holy Spirit, and a life in Christ Jesus.

## The Power of the Blood

Oh, brother or sister, God wants you to know that He has a redemption for you through the blood of Jesus, a new birth unto righteousness, a change from darkness into light, from the power of Satan unto God. This blessed salvation through the blood of Jesus will free you from all the power of Satan and make you a joint-heir with Christ. Oh, this is a glorious inheritance that we have in Jesus Christ. Glory to God! Jesus was manifested in the flesh, manifested to destroy the works of the devil. Christ can make us overcomers, destroying the power and passion of sin and dwelling in us by His mighty power. He can so transform our lives that we will love righteousness and hate iniquity. And He can make us holy, because just as God dwelt in His Son by the power of the Holy Spirit, so God can dwell in us through Christ.

# The Abiding Spirit

I want you to see that we receive sonship because of Christ's obedience. And do not forget what the Scripture says: *"Though He was a Son, yet He learned obedience by the things which He suffered"* (Heb. 5:8). If you turn to the Scriptures, you will see how the people reviled Him and how they tried to kill Him by throwing Him over the cliff. But He passed through the midst of the whole crowd, and as soon as He got out, He saw a blind man and healed him. He was in the world but not of it.

It is lovely—it is divinely glorious—this power of the new creation, this birth unto righteousness by faith in the Atonement. It can transform you so that you can be in Jesus Christ and know that it is another power dominating, controlling, and filling you, and making you understand that though you are still in the body you are governed by the Spirit. Oh, to live in all the beauty of the glory and grandeur of the Holy Spirit!

## Changed by His Love

There is a constraining power in this Christ that causes you to know that it is different from anything else in the world. In Scripture it is called an *"unfeigned love"* (1 Pet. 1:22 KJV), a real and sincere love. This has a tremendously deep meaning. What is it, exactly? Beloved, Jesus will tell you what it is. It is a denunciation of yourself as the power of Christ lays hold of you. He loved you when you were yet a sinner (Rom. 5:8), and He seeks your love in return. It is an unfeigned love, a love that can stand ridicule, persecution, and slander, because it is a love brought about in you by the power of the Holy Spirit changing you from one state of glory to another. Christ is

79

King of Kings and Lord of Lords, and *"of His king-dom there will be no end"* (Luke 1:33). *"He shall see His seed, He shall prolong His days, and the pleasure of the LORD shall prosper in His hand"* (Isa. 53:10).

Oh, beloved, what a Christ we have at this very moment! I want you to see that there is nothing like Him. If you see Him today, you needy ones, and gaze at Him, you will be changed. As you look at Him, you will find that even your natural bodies will change. His strength will come into you, and you will be transformed. He is the God of the sinner; He is the God of the helpless; He is full of mercy. I like the thought of His calling Himself the God of Jacob. When He says He is the God of Jacob, there is room for everybody. I tell you, He is your God, and He is preparing to meet you exactly as He met Jacob.

Jacob had deceived someone in everything he had done. He had deceived Esau to get his birthright (Gen. 25:29–34) and Laban to get his cattle (Gen. 30:25–43). Truly, the devil manipulated Jacob, but, praise God, there was one thing that Jacob knew: he knew that God had fulfilled His promise. In Bethel, God let Jacob see the ladder—a wonderful ladder, for it reached from earth to heaven—and Jacob saw the angels ascending and descending upon it. Bethel is the place of prayer, the place of changing conditions, of earth entering heaven. God brought Jacob right back to the same place, regardless of how he had wandered. Jacob had to let everything go, and he was left alone. The same old Jacob remained, and as long as God would let him wrestle with Him, he wrestled.

This is an example of holding on to this world—we never let go until we have to. God touched Jacob, and as soon as he was touched, he found out that he was no good. Then the Man said, *"Let Me go."* But Jacob answered, *"I will not let You go unless You bless me!"* (Gen. 32:26). Brother, God will bless you if you get to that point, but you are no good as long as you wrestle. When you come in helplessness and with a real cry of brokenness, then God will meet you. It is marvelous how God meets us in our distresses. When the cry comes from broken hearts, then God comes.

## His Mercy Endures

It is so lovely to know that God's mercy never fails. When Jesus came down from the Mount of Transfiguration, He set His face to go to the cross for you and me. When He came down from the mountain, there was a man there who had a son whom the devil had taken and thrown down and bruised. The man cried out, saying, "Lord, come and help me. Here is my son; the devil takes him and tears at him until he foams at the mouth. I brought him to Your disciples, but they could not help him." (See Mark 9:17–18.)

Oh, brother, may God strengthen our hands and take away all our unbelief. Jesus said, *"O faithless generation, how long shall I be with you?...Bring him to Me"* (v. 19), and they brought him to Jesus, who cast out the evil spirit. But even in the presence of Jesus, those evil spirits tore the boy and left him as one dead until Christ lifted him up. (See verses 20–27.)

Just think of that satanic power. The devil goes about to kill, *"seeking whom he may devour"* (1 Pet. 5:8), but Christ said, "I came to give life, and life

81

more abundantly." (See John 10:10.) May God keep us in the place where the devil will have no power and no victory. I pray God that the demon powers that come out of people in today's churches will never return again.

## Filled with the Spirit

Oh, if I could only show you what it means to be delivered by the power of Jesus and what it means to lose your deliverance through your own foolishness! I know of a case like this. A man possessed by demonic power and sickness and weakness came to Jesus, and He cast the evil spirit out. The man was made whole. Then, instead of the man seeking the Holy Spirit and the light of God, he afterward went to the races. God save us! The healing power is for the glory of God, and it appears that this man was *"swept, and put in order"* (Matt. 12:44), but he did not receive Christ and the power of the Spirit. So the evil spirit went back and found he could gain an entrance again because the man had no other inhabitant in him. He took with him other evil spirits, and the man's case was worse than before. (See verses 43–45.)

If you want to be healed by the power of God, it means that your life has to be filled with God. We must make sure that the power of God comes to inhabit us. Are you willing to so surrender yourself to God today that Satan will have no dominion over you?

# Five

# Looking toward Our Translation

 od has a plan for us in this life of the Spirit. We are to go and speak *"all the words of this life"* (Acts 5:20), this abundant life. Jesus came so that we might have life (John 10:10). Satan comes to steal and kill and destroy (v. 10), but God has for us abundance in full measure, pressed down, shaken together, and overflowing (Luke 6:38). God is filling us with His own personality and His presence, making us salt and light and glory, as a revelation of Himself. God is with us in all circumstances, afflictions, persecutions; in every one of our trials, He is girding us with truth. Christ the Initiative, the Triune God, is in control, and our every thought, word, and action must be in line with Him, with no weakness or failure. Our God is a God of might, light, and revelation, preparing us for heaven. *"Your life is hidden with Christ in God. When Christ who is our life appears, then you also will appear with Him in glory"* (Col. 3:3–4).

> *For we know that if our earthly house, this tent, is destroyed, we have a building from*

# Smith Wigglesworth on Heaven

*God, a house not made with hands, eternal in the heavens. For in this we groan, earnestly desiring to be clothed with our habitation which is from heaven, if indeed, having been clothed, we shall not be found naked. For we who are in this tent groan, being burdened, not because we want to be unclothed, but further clothed, that mortality may be swallowed up by life. Now He who has prepared us for this very thing is God, who also has given us the Spirit as a guarantee.* (2 Cor. 5:1–5)

God's Word is a tremendous word, a productive word that produces things like itself. It is power, producing Godlikeness. We get to heaven through the Word of God, and we have peace through the blood of His cross. Redemption is ours through the knowledge of the Word. I am saved because God's Word says so. *"If you confess with your mouth the Lord Jesus and believe in your heart that God has raised Him from the dead, you will be saved"* (Rom. 10:9).

If I am baptized with the Holy Spirit, it is because Jesus said, *"You shall receive power when the Holy Spirit has come upon you"* (Acts 1:8). We must have one thing in mind, and that is to be filled with the Holy Spirit, to be filled with God.

## Interpretation of Tongues

God has sent His Word to free us from the law of sin and death. Unless we die, we cannot live, and unless we cease to be, God cannot be.

## Looking toward Our Translation

### The Importance of Faith

The Holy Spirit has a royal plan, a heavenly plan. He came to unveil the King, to show the character of God, to unveil the precious blood. Since I have the Holy Spirit within me, I see Jesus clothed for humanity. He was moved by the Spirit and led by the Spirit. We read of some who heard the Word but did not benefit from it, because faith was lacking in them (Rom. 9:6–8). We must have a living faith in God's Word, a faith that is quickened by the Spirit.

A man may be saved and still have a human spirit. In many people who hear about the baptism of the Holy Spirit, the human spirit immediately arises against the Holy Spirit. The human spirit is not subject to the law of God, nor can it be. The disciples at one time wanted to call down fire from heaven, and Jesus said to them, *"You do not know what manner of spirit you are of"* (Luke 9:55). The human spirit is not subject to the law of God.

The Holy Spirit came forth for one purpose, and that was to reveal Jesus to us. Jesus *"made Himself of no reputation"* (Phil. 2:7), and He was obedient unto death (v. 8), that God should forever hold Him up as a token of submissive yieldedness. God highly exalted Him and gave Him a name above every name. *"Now He who has prepared us for this very thing is God, who also has given us the Spirit as a guarantee"* (2 Cor. 5:5). With the clothing upon of the Spirit, human depravity is covered, and everything that is contrary to the mind of God is destroyed. God must have bodies for Himself, perfectly prepared by the Holy Spirit, for the Day of the Lord.

*"For in this we groan, earnestly desiring to be clothed with our habitation which is from heaven"* (v. 2).

Was Paul speaking here about the coming of the Lord? No! Yet this condition of preparedness is highly relevant. The Holy Spirit is coming to take back a church and a perfect bride. The Holy Spirit must find in us perfect yieldedness, with every human desire subjected to Him. *"No one can say that Jesus is Lord except by the Holy Spirit"* (1 Cor. 12:3). He has come to reveal Christ in us, so that the glorious flow of the life of God may bring rivers of living water to the thirsty land within.

*"If Christ is in you, the body is dead because of sin, but the Spirit is life because of righteousness"* (Rom. 8:10).

### Interpretation of Tongues

This is that which God has declared freedom from the law. If we love the world, the love of the Father is not in us.

*"For all that is in the world; the lust of the flesh, the lust of the eyes, and the pride of life; is not of the Father but is of the world"* (1 John 2:16).

The Spirit has to breathe into us a new occupancy, a new order. The Holy Spirit came to give the vision of a life in which Jesus is perfected. It is Christ

> who has saved us and called us with a holy calling, not according to our works, but according to His own purpose and grace which was given to us in Christ Jesus before time began, but has now been revealed by the appearing of our Savior Jesus Christ, who has

# Looking toward Our Translation

*abolished death and brought life...through the gospel.* (2 Tim. 1:9–10)

We who are saved have been called with a holy calling, called to be saints—to be pure, holy, and Godlike; to be sons with power. It is a long time now since it was settled and death was abolished. Death has no more power. This was made known through the Gospel, which brought in immortality. Mortality is a hindrance. Sin has no more dominion over you. You reign in Christ, and you make rightful use of His finished work. Don't groan and travail for a week. If you are in need, *"only believe"* (Mark 5:36). Don't fast to get some special thing, *"only believe."* It is according to your faith that God blesses you with more faith. *"Have faith in God"* (Mark 11:22). If you are free in God, believe! Believe, and it will be unto you even as you believe. (See Matthew 9:29.)

*"Awake, you who sleep"* (Eph. 5:14); put on light, and open your eyes. *"If then you were raised with Christ, seek those things which are above, where Christ is, sitting at the right hand of God"* (Col. 3:1). Stir yourselves up, beloved! Where are you? I am risen with Christ, planted in Him. It was a beautiful planting. I am seated with Him. God gives me the credit, and I believe Him. Why should I doubt?

## Interpretation of Tongues

Why do you doubt when faith reigns? God makes it possible. How many people have received the Holy Spirit, and Satan gets a doubt in? Don't doubt, believe! There is power and strength in God. Who dares to believe in God?

# Smith Wigglesworth on Heaven

Leave Doubting Street; live on Faith-Victory Street. Jesus sent the seventy out, and they came back in victory (Luke 10:1–17). It takes God to make it real. Dare to believe until there is not a sick person, until there is no sickness, until everything is withered and the life of Jesus is implanted within your soul. *"The righteous will hold to his way"* (Job 17:9). God has reserved him who is godly for Himself (Ps. 4:3). Therefore, lift up your heads. The devil makes you remember the day you failed, though you would give the world to forget about it. But God has forgotten when He forgives. He forgets.

## Filled with the Spirit

God wants to make us pillars: honorable, strong, and holy. God will move us on. I am enamored with the possibility of this. God wants you to know that you are saved, cleansed, delivered, and marching to victory. He has given you the faith to believe. God has a plan for you! *"Set your mind on things above"* (Col. 3:2), and get into the heavenly places with Christ. *"Do not be conformed to this world, but be transformed by the renewing of your mind"* (Rom. 12:2).

You cannot repeat the name of Jesus too often. What a privilege it is to kneel and get right into heaven the moment we pray, where the glory descends, the fire burns, faith is active, and the light dispels the darkness. What is darkness? What is mortality? Mortality hinders, but the life of Jesus eats up mortality.

The book of Acts deals with receiving the Holy Spirit, and the epistles were written to believers who had been baptized in the Spirit. When I was in New

Zealand, some believers came to me, questioning the baptism of the Holy Spirit. They quoted from the epistles, but before we may be in the experience of the epistles, we must go through the Acts of the Apostles. I asked them, according to 1 Corinthians 14:2, "When did you speak in mysteries?" But they had not yet come into the baptism of the Holy Spirit.

Jesus is the light and the life of men; no man can have this light and still walk in darkness. *"When Christ who is our life appears, then you also will appear with Him in glory"* (Col. 3:4). Where His life is, disease cannot remain. Is not He who dwells in us greater than all? Is He greater? Yes, when He has full control. If one thing is permitted outside the will of God, it hinders us in our standing against the powers of Satan. We must allow the Word of God to judge us, lest we stand condemned with the world.

*"When Christ who is our life appears."* Can I have any life apart from Him, any joy or any fellowship apart from Him? Jesus said, *"The ruler of this world is coming, and he has nothing in Me"* (John 14:30). All that is contrary in us is withered by the indwelling life of the Son of God.

> *For we who are in this tent groan, being burdened, not because we want to be unclothed, but further clothed, that mortality may be swallowed up by life.*　　　(2 Cor. 5:4)

Are we ready? Have we been clothed with the Holy Spirit? Has mortality been swallowed up in life? If He who is our life came, we should go. I know the Lord. I know that the Lord laid His hand on me. He filled me with the Holy Spirit.

# Smith Wigglesworth on Heaven

I know that the Lord laid His hand on me. It is heaven on earth. Heaven has begun with me. I am happy now, and free, since the Comforter has come. The Comforter is the great Revealer of the kingdom of God. He came to give us the more abundant life. God has designed the plan, and nothing else really matters if the Lord loves us. God sets great store in us. The pure in heart see God. There are no stiff knees, coughing, or pain in the Spirit. Nothing ails us if we are filled with the Spirit.

> *If the Spirit of Him who raised Jesus from the dead dwells in you, He who raised Christ from the dead will also give life to your mortal bodies through His Spirit who dwells in you.*
> (Rom. 8:11)

The way into glory is through the flesh being torn away from the world and separated unto God. This freedom of spirit, freedom from the law of sin and death, is cause for rejoicing every day. The perfect law destroys the natural law. Spiritual activity takes in every passing ray, ushering in the days of heaven upon earth, when there is no sickness and when we do not even remember that we have bodies. The life of God changes us and brings us into the heavenly realm, where our reign over principalities and over all evil is limitless, powerful, and supernatural.

If the natural body decays, the Spirit renews. Spiritual power increases until, with one mind and one heart, the glory is brought down over all the earth, right on into divine life. When the whole life is filled, this is Pentecost come again. The life of the

Lord will be manifested wherever we are, whether in a bus or on a train. We will be filled with the life of Jesus unto perfection, rejoicing in hope of the glory of God (Rom. 5:2), always looking for our translation into heaven. The life of the Lord in us draws us as a magnet, with His life eating up all else.

I must have the overflowing life in the Spirit. God is not pleased with anything less. It is a disgrace to be part of an ordinary plan after we are filled with the Holy Spirit. We are to be salt in the earth, not lukewarm (Rev. 3:16). We are to be hot, which means seeing God with eagerness, liberty, movement, and power. Believe! Believe! Amen.

Six

# The Appointed Hour:
# Life out of Death

he communion service is a very blessed time for us to gather together in remembrance of the Lord. I want to remind you of this fact, that this is the only service we render to the Lord. All other services we attend are for us to get a blessing from the Lord, but Jesus said, *"Do this in remembrance of Me"* (Luke 22:19). We have gathered together to commemorate that wonderful death, victory, triumph, and the looking forward to the glorious hope. And I want you, if it is possible at all, to get rid of your religion.

It has been so-called religion at all times that has slain and destroyed what was good. When Satan entered into Judas, the only people whom the devil could speak to through Judas were the priests, sad as it is to say. They conspired to get him to betray Jesus, and the devil took money from these priests to put Jesus to death. Now, it is a very serious thing, for we must clearly understand whether we are of the right spirit or not, for no man can be of the Spirit of Christ and persecute another; no man can have the true Spirit of Jesus and slay his brother, and no man can follow the Lord Jesus and have enmity in his heart. You cannot have Jesus and have bitterness and hatred, and persecute the believer.

It is possible for us, if we are not careful, to have within us an evil spirit of unbelief, and even in our best state it is possible for us to have enmity unless we are perfectly dead and we allow the life of the Lord to lead us. Remember how Jesus wanted to pass through a certain place as He was going to Jerusalem. Because He would not stop and preach to them concerning the kingdom, they refused to allow Him to go through their section of the country. And the disciples who were with Jesus said to Him, *"Lord, do You want us to command fire to come down from heaven and consume them, just as Elijah did?"* (Luke 9:54). But Jesus turned and said, *"You do not know what manner of spirit you are of"* (v. 55). There they were, following Jesus and with Him all the time, but Jesus rebuked that spirit in them.

I pray God that you will get this out of this service: that our knowledge of Jesus is pure love, and pure love for Jesus is death to self on all accounts—body, soul, and the human spirit. I believe that if we are in the will of God, we will be perfectly directed at all times, and if we desire to know anything about the mighty works of Christ, we will have to follow what Jesus said. Whatever He said came to pass.

## Knowing the Mind of God

Many things happened in the lives of the apostles to show His power over all flesh. In regard to paying taxes, Jesus said to Peter, "We are free, we can enter into the city without paying tribute; nevertheless, we will pay." (See Matthew 17:24–27.) I like that thought, that Jesus was so righteous on all lines. It helps me a great deal. Then Jesus told Peter to do a very hard thing. He said, "Take that hook and cast it into the sea. Draw out a fish, and take from its gills a piece of silver for you and Me" (v. 27).

This was one of the hardest things Peter had to do. He had been fishing all his life, but never had he taken a coin out of a fish's mouth. There were thousands and millions of fish in the sea, but one fish had to have money in it. He went down to the sea as any natural man would, speculating and thinking, "How can it be?" But how could it not be, if Jesus said it would be? Then the perplexity would arise, "But there are so many fish! Which fish has the money?" Believer, if God speaks, it will be as He says. What you need is to know the mind of God and the Word of God, and you will be so free that you will never find a frown on your face or a tear in your eye.

The more you know of the mightiness of revelation, the more every fear will pass away. To know God is to be in the place of triumph. To know God is to be in the place of rest. To know God is to be in the place of victory. Undoubtedly, many things were in Peter's mind that day, but thank God there was one fish that had the silver piece, and Peter obeyed. Sometimes, to obey in blindness brings the victory. Sometimes, when perplexities arise in your mind, obedience means God working out the problem. Peter cast the hook into the sea, and it would have been amazing if you could have seen the disturbance the other fish made to move out of the way, all except the right one. God wanted just one among the millions of fish. God may put His hand upon you in the midst of millions of people, but if He speaks to you, the thing that He says will be appointed.

On this same occasion, Jesus said to Peter and the others that when they went out into the city they would see a man bearing a pitcher of water, and they should follow him (Mark 14:13). In those days, it was not customary in the East for men to carry anything on their heads. The women always did the carrying, but this had to be a man, and he had to have a pitcher.

I know of one preacher who said that it was quite all right for Jesus to arrange for a colt to be tied before He ever instructed His disciples to go and find it. Another preacher said it was quite easy for Jesus to feed those thousands of people with the five loaves, because the loaves in those days were so tremendously big, but he didn't say that it was a little boy who had been carrying the five loaves. Unbelief can be very blind, but faith can see through a stone wall. Faith, when it is moved by the power of God, can laugh when trouble is near.

The disciples said to the man with the pitcher, *"Where is the guest room?"* (v. 14). "How strange it is that you should ask," the man must have replied. "I have been preparing that room, wondering who needed it." When God is leading, it is marvelous how perfectly everything works into the plan. He was arranging everything. You think He cannot do that today for you? For you who have been in perplexities for days and days, God knows how to deliver you out of trouble; He knows how to be with you in the dark hour. He can make all things work together for good to those who love Him (Rom. 8:28). He has a way of arranging His plan, and when God comes in,

96

# The Appointed Hour: Life out of Death

you always know it was a day in which you lived in Him.

Oh, to live in God! There is a vast difference between living in God and living in speculation and hope. There is something better than hope, something better than speculation. *"The people who know their God shall be strong, and carry out great exploits"* (Dan. 11:32), and God wants us to know Him.

## The Appointed Hour

*"When the hour had come, He sat down, and the twelve apostles with Him"* (Luke 22:14). *"When the hour had come"*—that was the most wonderful hour. There never was an hour, never will be an hour like that hour. What hour was it? It was an hour when all of creation passed under the blood, when all that ever lived came under the glorious covering of the blood. It was an hour of destruction of demon power. It was an appointed hour of life coming out of death. It was an hour when all the world was coming into emancipation by the blood. It was an hour in the world's history when it emerged from dark chaos. It was a wonderful hour! Praise God for that hour! Was it a dark hour? It was a dark hour for Him, but a wonderful light dawned for us. It was tremendously dark for the Son of Man, but, praise God, He came through it.

There are some things in the Scriptures that move me greatly. I am glad that Paul was a human being. I am glad that Jesus became a man. I am glad that Daniel was human, and I am also glad that John was human. You ask, "Why?" Because I see that whatever God has done for other people, He can do for me. And I find that God has done such wonderful things for other people that I am always expecting that these things are possible for me. Think about this. It is a wonderful thought to me.

Jesus said in that trying hour—hear it for a moment—*"With fervent desire I have desired to eat this Passover with you before I suffer"* (Luke 22:15). Desire? What could be His desire? It was His desire because of the salvation of the world, His desire because of the dethronement of the powers of Satan, His desire because He knew He was going to conquer everything and make every man free who ever lived. It was a great desire, but what lay between Him and its fulfillment? Gethsemane lay between that and the cross!

Some people say that Jesus died on the cross. It is perfectly true, but is that the only place? Jesus also died in Gethsemane. That was the tragic moment! That was the place where He paid the debt. It was in Gethsemane, and Gethsemane was between Him and the cross. He had a desire to eat this Passover, and He knew that Gethsemane was between Him and the cross.

I want you to think about Gethsemane. There, alone and with the tremendous weight and the awful effect of all sin and disease upon that body, He cried out, *"If it is possible, let this cup pass from Me"* (Matt. 26:39). He could only save men when He was man, but here, like a giant who has been refreshed and is coming out of a great chaos of darkness, He comes forth: *"For this cause I was born"* (John 18:37). It was His purpose to die for the world.

Oh, believer, will it ever pass through your lips or your mind for a moment that you will not have a desire to serve Christ like that? Can you, under any circumstances, stoop to take up your cross fully, to be in the place of ridicule, to surrender anything for the Man who said He desired to eat the Passover with His disciples, knowing what it meant? It can only come out of the depths of love we have for Him that we can say right now, "Lord Jesus, I will follow You."

## Spiritual Revelation

Oh, brother or sister, there is something very wonderful in the decision in your heart! God knows the heart. You do not always have to be on the housetop and shout to indicate the condition of your heart. He knows your inward heart. You say, "I would be ashamed not to be willing to suffer for a Man who desired to suffer to save me." *"With fervent desire"* (Luke 22:15), He said.

I know what it is to have the kingdom of heaven within me. Jesus said that even the least in the kingdom of heaven is greater than John the Baptist (Matt. 11:11), meaning those who are under the blood, those who have seen the Lord by faith, those who know that by redemption they are made sons of God. I say to you, Jesus will never taste again until we are there with Him. The kingdom will never be complete—it could not be—until we are all there at that great Supper of the Lamb where there will be millions and trillions of the redeemed, which no man can count. We will be there when that Supper is taking place. I like to think of that.

I hope you will take one step into definite lines with God and believe it. It is an act of faith that God wants to bring you into, a perfecting of that love that will always avail. It is a fact that He has opened the kingdom of heaven to all believers and that He gives eternal life to those who believe. The Lord, the omnipotent God, knows the end from the beginning and has arranged by the blood of the Lamb to cover the guilty and to make intercession for all believers. Oh, it is a wonderful inheritance of faith to find shelter under the blood of Jesus!

I want you to see that He says, *"Do this in remembrance of Me"* (Luke 22:19). He took the cup, He took the bread, and He gave thanks. The very attitude of giving thanks for His shed blood, giving thanks for His broken body, overwhelms the heart. To think that my Lord could give thanks for His own shed blood! To think that my Lord could give thanks for His own broken body! Only divinity can reveal this sublime act unto the heart!

The natural man cannot receive this revelation, but the spiritual man, the man who has been created anew by faith in Christ, is open to it. The man who believes that God comes in has the eternal seed of truth and righteousness and faith born into him. From the moment that he sees the truth on the lines of faith, he is made a new creation. The flesh ceases; the spiritual man begins. One is taken off, and the other is taken on, until a man is in the presence of God. I believe that the Lord brings a child of faith into a place of rest, causes him to sit with Him in heavenly places, gives him a language in the Spirit, and makes him know that he no longer belongs to the law of creation.

Do you see the bread that represents His broken body? The Lord knew He could not bring us any nearer to His broken body. The body of Jesus was

# The Appointed Hour: Life out of Death

made of that bread, and He knew He could bring us no nearer. He took the natural elements and said, "This bread represents my broken body." (See Luke 22:19.) Now, will it ever become that body of Christ? No, never. You cannot make it so. It is foolishness to believe it, but I receive it as an emblem. When I eat it, the natural leads me into the supernatural, and instantly I begin to feed on the supernatural by faith. One leads me into the other.

Jesus said, *"Take, eat; this is My body"* (Matt. 26:26). I have a real knowledge of Christ through this emblem. May we take from the table of the riches of His promises. The riches of heaven are before us. Fear not, only believe, for God has opened the treasures of His holy Word.

As the disciples were all gathered together with Jesus, He looked on them and said right into their ears, *"One of you will betray Me"* (v. 21). Jesus knew who would betray Him. He had known it for many, many months. They whispered to one another, "Who is it?" None of them had real confidence that it would not be he. That is the serious part about it; they had so little confidence in their ability to face the opposition that was before them, and they had no confidence that it would not be one of them.

Jesus knew. I can imagine that He had been talking to Judas many times, rebuking him and telling him that his course would surely bring him to a bad end. Jesus never had told any of His disciples, not even John who *"leaned on His breast"* (John 21:20). Now, if that same spirit of keeping things secret was in any church, it would purify the church. But I fear sometimes that Satan gets the advantage, and things are told before they are true. I believe

101

# Smith Wigglesworth on Heaven

God wants to so sanctify us, so separate us, that we will have that perfection of love that will not speak ill of a brother, that we will not slander a fellow believer whether it is true or not.

There was strife among them as to who should be the greatest, but He said, *"He who is greatest among you, let him be as the younger, and he who governs as he who serves"* (Luke 22:26). Then He, the Master, said, *"I am among you as the One who serves"* (v. 27). He, the noblest, the purest, was the servant of all! Exercising lordship over another is not of God. We must learn in our hearts that fellowship, true righteousness, loving one another, and preferring one another, must come into the church. Pentecost must outreach everything that ever has been, and we know it will if we are willing.

## Moving toward Perfection

But it cannot be if we do not will it. We can never be filled with the Holy Spirit as long as there is any human craving for our own wills. Selfishness must be destroyed. Jesus was perfect, the end of everything, and God will bring us all there. It is giving that pays; it is helping that pays; it is loving that pays; it is putting yourself out for another person that pays.

> *I am among you as the One who serves. But you are those who have continued with Me in My trials. And I bestow upon you a kingdom, just as My Father bestowed one upon Me.*
>
> (Luke 22:27–29)

# The Appointed Hour: Life out of Death

I believe there is a day coming that will be greater than anything any of us have any conception of. This is the testing road. This is the place where your whole body has to be covered with the wings of God so that your nakedness will not be seen. This is the thing that God is getting you ready for, the most wonderful thing your heart can imagine. How can you get into it? First of all, *"You...have continued with Me in My trials"* (v. 28). Jesus had been in trials; He had been in temptation. There is not one of us who is tempted beyond what He was (Heb. 4:15).

If a young man can be so pure that he cannot be tempted, he will never be fit to be made a judge, but God intends us to be so purified during these evil days that He can make us judges in the world to come. If you can be tried, if you can be tempted on any line, Jesus said, *"You are those who have continued with Me in My trials"* (Luke 22:28). Have faith, and God will keep you pure in the temptation.

How will we reach it? In Matthew 19:28, Jesus said,

> *In the regeneration, when the Son of Man sits on the throne of His glory, you who have followed Me will also sit on twelve thrones, judging the twelve tribes of Israel.*

Follow Him in constant regeneration. Every day is a regeneration; every day is a day of advancement; every day is a place of choice. Every day you find yourself in need of fresh consecration. If you are in a place to yield, God moves you in the place of regeneration.

# Smith Wigglesworth on Heaven

For years and years God has been making me appear to hundreds and thousands of people as a fool. I remember the day when He saved me and when He called me out. If there is a thing God wants to do today, He wants to be as real to you and me as He was to Abraham. After I was saved, I joined a church that consisted of a very lively group of people who were full of a revival spirit, and it was marvelous how God blessed us. And then there came a lukewarmness and indifference, and God said to me as clearly as anything, "Come out." I obeyed and came out. The people said, "We cannot understand you. We need you now, and you are leaving us."

The Plymouth Brethren at that time were in a conference. The Word of God was with them in power; the love of God was with them unveiled. Baptism by immersion was revealed to me, and when my friends saw me go into the water, they said I was altogether wrong. But God had called me, and I obeyed. The day came when I saw that the people of that church had dropped down to the letter of the law, only the letter, dry and barren.

At that time the Salvation Army was filled with love, filled with power, filled with zeal; every place was a revival, and I joined up with them. For about six years, the glory of God was there, and then the Lord said again, "Come out," and I was glad I came. It dropped right into a social movement, and God has no place for a social movement. We are saved by regeneration, and the man who is going on with God has no time for social reforms.

God moved on, and at that time there were many people who were receiving the baptism of the Holy Spirit without signs. Those days were days of heaven on earth. God unfolded the truth, showed the way of sanctification by the power of the blood of Christ, and in that I saw the great inflow of the life of God.

I thank God for that, but God came along again and said, "Come out." I obeyed God and went with what others called the "tongues folks"; they were regarded as having further light. I saw God orchestrating every movement I made, and even in this Pentecostal work, unless we see there is a real death, I can see that God will say to us, "Come out." Unless Pentecostalism wakes up to shake herself free from all worldly things and comes into a place of divine likeness with God, we will hear the voice of God saying, "Come out." He will have something far better than this.

I ask every one of you, Will you hear the voice of God and come out? You ask, "What do you mean?" Every one of you, without exception, knows that the only meaning of Pentecost is being on fire. If you are not on fire, you are not in the place of regeneration. It is only the fire of God that burns up the entanglements of the world.

When we came into this new work, God spoke to us by the Spirit, and we knew we had to reach the place of absolute yieldedness and cleansing, so that there would be nothing left. We were *"swept, and put in order"* (Matt. 12:44). Believer, that was only the beginning, and if you have not made tremendous progress in that holy zeal and power and compassion of God, we can truly say you have backslidden in heart. The backslider in heart is dead. He does not have the open vision. The backslider in heart does not see the Word of God in a fresher light every day.

You can say that a man is a backslider in heart if he is not hated by the world. If you have the applause of the world, you do not have the approval of God.

## A Place Prepared for You

I do not know whether you will receive it or not, but my heart burns with the message of changing in the regeneration, for when you are changed, you will get a place in the kingdom to come where you will be in authority. This is the place that God has prepared for us, the place that is beyond all human conception. We can catch a glimpse of this glory when we see how John worshipped the angel, and the angel said to him, *"See that you do not do that! I am your fellow servant, and of your brethren who have the testimony of Jesus"* (Rev. 19:10). This angel was showing John the wonders of the glorious kingdom, and in the angel's glorified state, John thought the angel was the Lord. I wonder if we dare believe for it.

Let me close with these words: *"As we have borne the image of the man of dust, we shall also bear the image of the heavenly Man"* (1 Cor. 15:49). To us, this means that everything of an earthly type has to cease, for the heavenly type is so wonderful in all its purity. God is full of love, full of purity, full of power. But there is no power in purity itself! There is no open door into heaven only on the basis of the void of sin between man and God. The heavens open only where the Spirit of the Lord is so leading that flesh has no power. But we will live in the Spirit. God bless you and prepare you for greater days.

Seven

# The Bread of Life

he Lord has revealed to me a new order concerning the Word of God. It is called the Book of Life. It is called the Spirit of Life. It is called the Son of Life, the Word of Life, the testament of the new covenant, which has been shed in blood. Here it is, the Bible. I hold it before you, and it is no more than any other book without the Spirit of revelation. It is a dead letter; it is lifeless. It has no power to give regeneration; it has no power to cause new creation; it has no power to cause the new birth apart from the Spirit; it is only words printed on the page. But as the Spirit of the Lord is upon us and in us, we breathe the very nature of the life of the new creation, and it becomes a quickened book. It becomes a life-giving source; it becomes the breath of the Almighty; it becomes to us a new order in the Spirit.

### Interpretation of Tongues

We will not die, but we will live to declare the works of the Lord (Ps. 118:17). We have passed from death unto life; we are a new creation in the Spirit. We are born of a new nature; we are quickened by a new power; we belong to a new association. Our citizenship is in heaven, from which we look for our nature, our Life, our All in All.

That is beautiful! The Spirit is moving, giving, speaking, and making life! Can't you hear the Master say, "My Word is spirit and life"? (See John 6:63.) Only by the Spirit can we understand what is spiritual. We cannot understand it on our own. We have to be spiritual to understand it. No man can understand the Word of God without his being quickened by the new nature. The Word of God is for the new nature. The Word of God is for the new life, to quicken mortal flesh.

Note these words from the gospel of John:

*Most assuredly, I say to you, he who believes in Me has everlasting life. I am the bread of life. Your fathers ate the manna in the wilderness, and are dead. This is the bread which comes down from heaven, that one may eat of it and not die.* (John 6:47–50)

I hope you have this everlasting life, for I can tell you that it has changed me already. It is all new. The Word of God is never stale; it is all life. May we be so spiritually minded that it becomes life and truth to us.

Christ said, *"I am the living bread"* (v. 51). Living bread! Oh, can't you feel it? Couldn't you just eat it? Your gums will never be sore, and your teeth will never ache eating this bread. The more you eat, the more you will have life, and it won't wear your body out, either. Instead, it will quicken your mortal body (Rom. 8:11). This is the Living Bread. Feed on it, believe it, digest it. Let it have a real, new quickening in your body.

I could sit and listen to anybody read these verses all day, and I could eat it all day. Living bread! Eternal bread! Eternal life! Oh, the brightening of the countenance, the joy of the new nature, the hope that thrills us, and the bliss that awaits us when we eat of this Living Bread! The glory of it will never decay.

## On the Way to Heaven

We long for that eternal day when all are holy, all are good, all are washed in Jesus' blood. But guilty, unrenewed sinners cannot come there. There is no sickness in heaven. There is no death in heaven. They have never had a funeral in that land. They have never known what it means to ring the death toll or to have the drum muffled. Never once has anyone died up there. There is no death there, no sickness, no sorrow.

Will you go there? Are you getting ready for it?

Remember this: you were created by the power of God for one purpose in particular. God had no thought in Creation but to bring forth through mortality a natural order so that you might be quickened in the Spirit, be received into glory, and worship God in a way that the angels never could. But in order for that to be, He has brought us through the flesh and quickened us by the Spirit, so that we may know the love, the grace, the power, and all the perfect will of God.

He is a wonderful God—His intelligence, His superabundance in all revelation, His power to keep everything in perfect order. The sun in all its glory, shining so majestically on the earth today, is the mighty power of our glorious God who can make a new heaven and a new earth, in which righteousness will dwell, where no sin will ever darken the place, where the glory of that celestial place will be wonderful.

> *I, John, saw the holy city, New Jerusalem, coming down out of heaven from God, prepared as a bride adorned for her husband.*
> (Rev. 21:2)

This city—figurative, but not exactly figurative, for it is a luminous fact—will surely exist, and we cannot miss it. It will be a city greater than any city ever known, with millions, billions, trillions all ready for the marriage of the Lamb and His bride. It will make a great city—architecture, domes, pinnacles, cornices, foundations—and the whole city will be made up of saints coming to a marriage.

Oh, the glory of it! I'll be there. I will be one of its inhabitants. I do not know what part, but it will be glorious to be in it anyhow. All these billions of people will have come through tribulation, distress, brokenness of spirit, hard times, strange perplexities, weariness, and all kinds of conditions in the earth. They will be quickened and made like Him, to reign with Him forever and ever.

What a thought God had when He was forming creation and making it, so that we could bring forth sons and daughters in the natural, who are quickened by the Spirit in the supernatural and received up to glory, to be made ready for a marriage! May

# The Bread of Life

God reveal to us our position in this Holy Spirit order, so that we may see how wonderful it is that the Lord has His mind upon us. I want you to see security, absolute security, where there will be no shaking, no trembling, no fear, absolute soundness in every way, knowing that, as sure as the Celestial City is formed, you are going to that City.

Salvation takes us to glory. New life is resurrection, it is ascension, and this new life in God has no place for its feet anywhere between here and glory.

The Spirit of the Lord is with us, revealing the Word. He does not bring eternal life to us, for we have that already, and we believe and are in this place because of that eternal life. But He brings to us a process of this eternal life, showing us that it puts everything else to death. Eternal life came to us when we believed, but the process of eternal life can begin today, making us know that now we are sons of God.

## Interpretation of Tongues

Let your whole heart be in a responsive place. Yield absolutely to the Spirit's cry within you. Do not be afraid of being so harmonized by the power of the Spirit that the Spirit in you becomes so one with you that you are altogether what He desires you to be.

Do not let fear in any way come in. Let the harmonizing, spiritual life of God breathe through you that oneness, and when we get into oneness today, oh, the lift, oh, the difference will be great! When our hearts are all blended in one thought, how the Spirit lifts us, how revelation can come! God is ready to take us far beyond anything we have had before.

# Smith Wigglesworth on Heaven

Notice some more verses in the sixth chapter of John:

> *The Jews therefore quarreled among themselves, saying, "How can this Man give us His flesh to eat?" Then Jesus said to them, "Most assuredly, I say to you, unless you eat the flesh of the Son of Man and drink His blood, you have no life in you. Whoever eats My flesh and drinks My blood has eternal life, and I will raise him up at the last day. For My flesh is food indeed, and My blood is drink indeed. He who eats My flesh and drinks My blood abides in Me, and I in him."* (John 6:52–56)

There is another passage that is very lovely in the fourth chapter of the first epistle of John: *"He who abides in love abides in God, and God in him"* (v. 16). You cannot separate these divine personalities. If you begin to separate the life from the nature, you will not know where you are. You will have to see that the new nature is formed right in you.

## Resurrection Power

You get a glimpse of it in a very clear way in Hebrews 4:12. The Word of God—the Word, the Life, the Son, the Bread, the Spirit—is in you, separating you from soulishness. The same power, the same Spirit, separates soul and spirit, joint and marrow, right in you. The Life, the Word, is the same power that by the Spirit quickens the mortal body. It is resurrection force; it is divine order. The stiff knee, the inactive limb, the strained position of the back, the muscles, and everything in your nature takes on resurrection power by the Word, the living Word in the body, discerning, opening, and revealing the hidden thoughts of the heart until the heart cannot have one thing that is contrary to God. The heart is separated in thought and in life until the whole man is brought into divine life, living in this life, moving by this power, quickened by this principle.

Oh, this is resurrection! This is resurrection! Is it anything else? Yes, this is what will leave us.

I do not know how far this goes, but I am told that when the spiritual life of a man is very wonderfully active, his white blood cells are very mightily quickened as they are going through the body. However, after the spirit goes, these cells cannot be found in any way. I do not know how far that goes, but to me, it is a reality; the Spirit of the living God flows through every vein of my body, through every tissue of my blood, and I know that this life will have to go. It will have to go!

### Interpretation of Tongues

"It is not by might or power; it is by my Spirit," says the Lord. (See Zechariah 4:6.) It is not the letter, but it is the Spirit that quickens. It is the resurrection that He brought into us. "I am the resurrection and the life. He who believes in Me has resurrection life in him, resurrection power through him, and he will decrease and the resurrection will increase." (See John 11:25.)

May God manifest that through us and give us that. Oh, how I yearn for this spiritual, divine appointment for us today, to see this deep, holy, inward reviving in our hearts!

I must press on. I am pressing on. The only difficulty is, God is pressing in and keeping us in, holding on but laying hold. Not until these last days have I been able to understand Paul's words to Timothy when he told him he was to lay hold of eternal life. We cannot imagine any human being in the world laying hold of eternal life—it never could be—but a supernatural human being has the power to lay hold, to take hold. Thus, it is the supernatural and divine that lays hold, laying hold of eternal life.

Eternal life, which was with the Father, was brought to us by the Son and is of Him. *"As the living Father sent Me, and I live because of the Father, so he who feeds on Me will live because of Me"* (John 6:57).

Here is a divine principle. He had His life from the Father. "As I live by the Father and have life in Myself by the Father, so you will live by Me and have life from Me as I take it from the Father." Oh, that the Lord would inspire thought and revelation in our hearts to claim this today!

*"This is the bread which came down from heaven; not as your fathers ate the manna, and are dead. He who eats of this bread will live forever"* (v. 58). The manna was wonderful bread. It was a wonderful provision; but the people ate it, and they still died. But God's Son became the Bread of Life, and as we eat of this Bread, we live forever!

### Interpretation of Tongues

It is the Spirit who gives life, for He gives His life for us so that we, being dead, might have eternal life. For He came to give us His own life, that we henceforth should not die, but live forever.

# The Bread of Life

## Living in the Spirit

Breathe upon us, breathe upon us,
With Thy love our hearts inspire:
Breathe upon us, breathe upon us,
Lord, baptize us now with fire.

Thank God for the breath of the Spirit, the new creation dawning. Thank God for the spiritual revelation. Fire, holy fire, burning fire, purging fire, taking the dross, taking everything out, making us pure gold. Fire! *"He will baptize you with the Holy Spirit and fire"* (Matt. 3:11). It is a burning that is different from anything else, a burning without consuming. It is illumining, an illumination different from anything else. It illumines the very nature of the man in such a way that in the inner recesses of his human nature there is a burning, holy, divine purging that goes on until every part of the dross is consumed. Carnality in all its darknesses, and the human mind with all its blotches, are inadequate to reach out and are destroyed by the fire. We will be burned by fire until the very purity of Christ is through and through and through, until the body is, as it were, consumed.

It seems to me the whole of the flesh of Jesus was finished up, was consumed in the Garden, on the cross, in His tragic moments. He was consumed when He spoke about seed falling to the ground (see John 12:24), and when He said in great agony, with sweat upon His brow, *"If it is possible, let this cup pass from Me; nevertheless, not as I will, but as You will"* (Matt. 26:39).

# Smith Wigglesworth on Heaven

There is a consuming of the flesh until the invisible becomes so mighty that what is visible will only hold its own for the invisible to come forth into the glorious, blessed position of God's sonship.

> *These things He said in the synagogue as He taught in Capernaum. Therefore many of His disciples, when they heard this, said, "This is a hard saying; who can understand it?"*
> (John 6:59–60)

It may be difficult for some of you to clearly understand this ministry we are giving you. Now, I tell you what to do: if you are not sitting in judgment but are allowing the Spirit to come forth to you, you will find out that even mysteries will be unfolded to you, and difficulties will be cleared up. These people sat in judgment without being willing to enter into the spiritual revelation of it. As you read the following verse, I want you to see how it divided the situation: *"When Jesus knew in Himself that His disciples complained about this, He said to them, 'Does this offend you?'"* (v. 61).

Jesus was a perceptive person. We, too, may get to the place where we rightly understand these things and can perceive whether people are receptive or not. I am immediately sensitive to the fact when there is anybody in a meeting or church service who is sitting in judgment of the meeting. Jesus felt this and said unto them,

> *Does this offend you? What then if you should see the Son of Man ascend where He was before? It is the Spirit who gives life; the flesh*

# The Bread of Life

*profits nothing. The words that I speak to you*
*are spirit, and they are life.*     (John 6: 61–63)

We have been having the Word, which is *"life"*
and *"spirit."* There is not a particle of your flesh that
will ever be of any advantage to you as long as you
live. It has pleased God to give you a body, but only
so that it may be able to contain the fullness of the
principles and life of the Godhead. (See Colossians
2:9.) Your body has only been given to you so that it
might be so quickened with a new generation of the
Spirit that you can pass through this world with salt
in your life, with seasoning qualities, with light divine, with a perfect position. He wants you walking
up and down the breadth of the land, overcoming the
powers of Satan, living in this spiritual relationship
with God until your body is only used to take the
*"spirit"* and the *"life"* from one quarter of the globe
to the other, quickened by the Spirit. The flesh never
had anything for you; the Spirit is the only property
that will help you any time. In my flesh there never
has been, there never will be, any good thing; the
body can only be the temple of the Holy One.

Oh, to live! "If I live, I live unto Christ; if I die, I
die unto Christ. Living or dying, I am the Lord's."
(See Romans 14:8.) This is a wonderful message
given to us by Paul, a saintly, holy, divine person,
full of holy richness. I want to say another thing
about this holy man, Paul, who was so filled with the
power of the Holy Spirit that the Spirit moved in his
mortal life until his flesh was torn to pieces with the
rocks. Though his fleshly body was all the time under great privation, the Spirit moved in his life. He
often came close to death, but he was quickened

117

again in the Spirit. He was laid out for dead but was again quickened and brought to life.

What a wonderful position! *"I am now ready to be offered"* (2 Tim. 4:6 KJV)—offered on the altar of sacrifice. By the mercy of God, Paul lived and moved by the Spirit, energized and filled with a power a million times larger than himself. He was imprisoned; he had infirmities and weaknesses and all kinds of trials, but the Spirit filled his human body; and in a climax, as it were, of soul and body mingled, he wrote the words, *"'I am now ready to be offered.'* There is the guillotine; *'I am now ready to be offered.'"* Already he had been on the altar of living sacrifice, and he taught us how to do the same.

But here he came to another sacrifice: *"I am now ready to be offered."* I do not know how it was, but I thank God he was ready to be offered. What a life! What a consummation. Human life was consummated, eaten up by the life of Another; mortality itself was eaten up until it did not have a vestige of the human nature to say, "You will not do that, Paul." What a consummation! What a holy invocation! What an entire separation! What a prospect of glorification!

Can it be? Yes, as surely as you are in the flesh, the same power of the quickening of the Spirit can come to you until, whether in your body or out of your body, you can only say, "I am not particular, as long as I know that

> Christ liveth in me!
> Christ liveth in me!
> Oh! what a salvation this,
> That Christ liveth in me."

# The Bread of Life

[Jesus said,] *"But there are some of you who do not believe." For Jesus knew from the beginning who they were who did not believe, and who would betray Him. And He said, "Therefore I have said to you that no one can come to Me unless it has been granted to him by My Father."* (John 6:64–65)

## Maintaining the Divine Life

It is so precisely divine in its origin that God will give this life only to those who attain unto eternal life. Do not get away from this. For every person who has eternal life, it is the purpose of the Father, it is the loyalty of God's Son, it is the assembly of the firstborn (Heb. 12:23), it is the newly begotten of God, it is the new creation, it is a race designed for heaven that is going to equip you and get you through everything. As surely as you are seeking now, you are in the glory. There is a bridge of eternal security for you if you dare to believe in the Word of God. There is not a drop between you and the glory. It is divine, it is eternal, it is holy, it is the life of God; He gives it, and no man can take from you the life that God gives to you.

This is wonderful! It is almightiness. Its production is absolutely unique. It is so essential, in the first place; it is so to be productive, in the next place; it is so to be changed, in the third place; it is so to be seated, in the fourth place. It is the nature of God that cannot rest in the earth. It is His nature from heaven. It is a divine nature. It is an eternal power. It is an eternal life. It belongs to heaven; it must go back from where it came.

# Smith Wigglesworth on Heaven

I hope no person will say, "Wigglesworth is preaching eternal security." I am not. I have a thousand times better things in my mind than that. My preaching is this: I know I have what will not be taken away from me. *"Mary has chosen that good part, which will not be taken away from her"* (Luke 10:42).

I am dwelling upon the sovereignty, the mercy, and the boundless love of God. I am dwelling upon the wonderful power of God's order. The heavens, the earth, and everything under the earth are submissive to the Most High God. Demon power has to give place to the royal kingship of God's eternal throne. *"Every knee shall bow"* (Isa. 45:23), every devil will be submitted, and God will bring us someday right into the fullness of the blaze of eternal bliss. And the brightness of His presence will cast every unclean spirit and every power of devils into the pit forever and ever and ever.

## Interpretation of Tongues

Why faint, then, at tribulation when these light afflictions, which are only for a moment, are working out for us an eternal, glorious weight of glory (2 Cor. 4:17)? For we see this: God, in His great plan of preparing, has delivered us from the corruption of the world and has transformed us and made us able to come into the image of the Most Holy One. We are made free from the law of sin and death because the life of Christ has been manifested in our mortal bodies (Rom. 8:2). Therefore, we live—and yet we live by another Life, another Power, an eternal Force, a resurrection glory.

# The Bread of Life

Oh, Jesus! If our fellowship here is so sweet, if the touches of the eternal glory move our inspiration, it must be wonderful to be there!

*From that time many of His disciples went back and walked with Him no more. Then Jesus said to the twelve, "Do you also want to go away?" But Simon Peter answered Him, "Lord, to whom shall we go? You have the words of eternal life."* (John 6:66–68)

Where will you go? If you leave the Master, where will you go? Where can we go? If we need a touch in our bodies, where can we go? If we want life, where can we go? Is there anywhere? This world is a big world, but tell me if you can get it.

Could you get it if you soared the heights of the Alps of Switzerland and looked over those glassy mountains where the sun is shining? As I looked over one of those mountains one morning, I saw eleven glaciers and three lakes, like diamonds before me in the glittering sun. I wept and I wept, but I did not get consolation. Then I dropped on my knees and looked to God—then I got consolation.

Where will we go? There are all the grandeurs and the glories of earth to be seen, but they do not satisfy me. They all belong to Time; they will all fold up like a garment that is laid aside; they will all melt with fervent heat (2 Pet. 3:10).

Where will we go? *"You have the words of eternal life"* (John 6:68). Jesus, You fed us with bread from heaven. Jesus, give us Your life. Oh, breathe it into us! Then we will eat and drink and breathe and think in God's Son until our own natures are eaten up with the divine life, until we are perpetually in the sweetness of His divine will and in the glory. In fact, we are already in it! Praise Him! You can always be holy; you can always be pure. It is the mind of the Spirit that is making you know holiness, righteousness, and rapture.

# Eight

# Changed from Glory to Glory

*Who also made us sufficient as ministers of the new
covenant, not of the letter but of the Spirit; for the
letter kills, but the Spirit gives life. But if the
ministry of death, written and engraved on
stones, was glorious, so that the children of Israel
could not look steadily at the face of Moses
because of the glory of his countenance,
which glory was passing away.*
—2 Corinthians 3:6–7

otice especially the seventh verse, where
we read that the glory that was on the
face of Moses had to pass away. Why was
it to be done away with? So that something else that had exceeding glory could
take its place.

> *For if the ministry of condemnation had glory,
> the ministry of righteousness exceeds much
> more in glory. For even what was made glori-
> ous had no glory in this respect, because of the
> glory that excels.* (vv. 9–10)

# Smith Wigglesworth on Heaven

I am positive that we have no conception of the depths and heights of the liberty and blessing of the *"ministry of the Spirit"* (v. 8). We must attain to this position of godliness, and we must be partakers of the divine nature (2 Pet. 1:4). The law was so glorious that Moses was filled with joy in the expectation of what it would mean. To us, there is the excellence of Christ's glory in the ministry of the Holy Spirit. *"In Him we live and move"* (Acts 17:28) and reign over all things. It is no longer, "Thou shalt not." Rather, it is God's will, revealed to us in Christ. *"I delight to do Your will, O my God"* (Ps. 40:8). And, beloved, in our hearts there is exceeding glory. Oh, the joy of this celestial touch!

When Peter was recalling that wonderful day on the Mount of Transfiguration, he said, *"Such a voice came to Him from the Excellent Glory: 'This is My beloved Son, in whom I am well pleased'"* (2 Pet. 1:17). If I were to come to you right now and say, "Whatever you do, you must try to be holy," I would miss it. I would be altogether outside of God's plan. But I take the words of the epistle, which says by the Holy Spirit, *"Be holy"* (1 Pet. 1:16). It is as easy as possible to be holy, but you can never be holy by your own efforts. When you lose your heart and Another takes your heart, and you lose your desires and He takes the desires, then you live in that sunshine of bliss that no mortal can ever touch. God wants us to be entirely eaten up by this holy zeal for Him, so that every day we will walk in the Spirit. It is lovely to walk in the Spirit, for He will cause you to dwell in safety, to rejoice inwardly, and to praise God reverently.

# Changed from Glory to Glory

## The Righteousness of Christ

*"The ministry of righteousness exceeds much more in glory"* (2 Cor. 3:9). I want to speak about righteousness now. You cannot touch this blessedness without saying that the excellent glory exceeds in Christ. All excellent glory is in Him; all righteousness is in Him. Everything that pertains to holiness and godliness, everything that denounces and brings to death the natural, everything that makes you know that you have forever ceased to be, is always in an endless power in the risen Christ.

Whenever you look at Jesus, you can see so many different facts of His life. I see Him in those forty days before His ascension, with wonderful truth, infallible proofs of His ministry. What was the ministry of Christ? When you come to the very essence of His ministry, it was the righteousness of His purpose. The excellence of His ministry was the glory that covered Him. His Word was convincing, inflexible, and divine, with a personality of an eternal endurance. It never failed. He spoke, and it stood fast. It was an immovable condition with Him, and His righteousness abides. God must bring us there: we must be people of our word, so that people will be able to depend upon our word.

Jesus was true, inwardly and outwardly. He is *"the way, the truth, and the life"* (John 14:6), and on this foundation we can build. When we know that our own hearts do not condemn us (1 John 3:21), we can say to the mountain, *"Be removed"* (Matt. 21:21). But when our own hearts do condemn us, there is no power in prayer, no power in preaching. We are just *"sounding brass or a clanging cymbal"*

(1 Cor. 13:1). May the Holy Spirit show us that there must be a ministry of righteousness.

Christ was righteousness through and through. He is lovely! Oh, truly, He is beautiful. God wants to fix it in our hearts that we are to be like Him—like Him in character. God wants righteousness in the inward parts, so that we may be pure through and through. The Bible is the plumb line of everything, and unless we are plumbed right up with the Word of God, we will fail in righteousness.

*"For even what was made glorious had no glory in this respect, because of the glory that excels"* (2 Cor. 3:10). You have to get right behind this blessed Word and say it is of God. Here, we come again to the law. I see that it was truly a schoolmaster that brought us to Christ (Gal. 3:24).

## Divinely Used by God

Law is beautiful when law is established in the earth. As far as possible in every country and town, you will find that the law has something to do with keeping things straight, and in a measure the city has some kind of sobriety because of the law. But, beloved, we belong to a higher, nobler citizenship, not an earthly citizenship, for *"our citizenship is in heaven"* (Phil. 3:20). If the natural law will keep an earthly city in somewhat moderate conditions, what will the excellent glory be in divine relationship to the citizenship to which we belong? What is meant by *excellent glory* is that it outshines. The earth is filled with broken hearts, but the excellent glory fills redeemed men and women so that they show forth the excellency of the grace of the glory of God.

# Changed from Glory to Glory

*Therefore, since we have such hope, we use great boldness of speech; unlike Moses, who put a veil over his face so that the children of Israel could not look steadily at the end of what was passing away.* (2 Cor. 3:12–13)

The man who is going on with God will have no mix-up in his oratory. He will be so plain and precise and divine in his speech, that everything will have a lift toward the glory. He must use great plainness of speech, but he must be a man who knows his message. He must know what God has in His mind in the Spirit, not in the letter. He is there as a vessel for honor, God's mouthpiece; therefore, he stands in the presence of God, and God speaks through him and uses him.

I always say that you cannot sing a song of victory in a minor key. If your life is not in constant pitch, you will never ring the bells of heaven. You must always be in tune with God, and then the music will come out as sweet as possible. We must be the mouthpiece of God, not by letter, but by the Spirit, and we must be so in the will of God that He will rejoice over us with singing (Zeph. 3:17). If we are in the Spirit, the Lord of life is the same Spirit. *"Now the Lord is the Spirit; and where the Spirit of the Lord is, there is liberty"* (2 Cor. 3:17).

There is no liberty that is going to help the people so much as testimony. I find people who do not know how to testify in the right way. We must testify only as the Spirit gives utterance. You are not to use your liberty except for the glory of God. So many meetings are spoiled by long prayers and long testimonies. If the speaker remains in the Spirit, he will know when he should sit down. When you begin to repeat yourself, the people get wearied, and they wish you would sit down, for the anointing has then ceased.

It is lovely to pray, and it is a joy to hear you pray when you are in the Spirit; but if you keep going after the Spirit has finished, all the people get tired of it. So God wants us to know that we are not to use liberty simply because we have it to use, but we are to let the liberty of the Spirit use us. Then we will know when to end. The meetings ought to be so free in the Spirit that people can always go away with the feeling, "Oh, I wish the meeting had gone on for another hour," or, "Was not that testimony meeting a revelation!"

The last verse I want to discuss from 2 Corinthians is the most glorious of all for us:

*But we all, with unveiled face, beholding as in a mirror the glory of the Lord, are being transformed into the same image from glory to glory, just as by the Spirit of the Lord.*
(2 Cor. 3:18)

So there is glory upon glory, and joy upon joy, and a measureless measure of joy and glory. Beloved, we get God's Word so wonderfully in our hearts that it absolutely changes us in everything. And as we so feast on the Word of the Lord, so eat and digest the truth, and inwardly eat of Christ, we are changed every day from one state of glory to another. You will never find anything else but the Word that takes you there, so you cannot afford to put aside that Word.

## Changed from Glory to Glory

I implore you, beloved, that you come short of none of these blessed teachings. These grand truths of the Word of God must be your testimony, must be your life, your pattern. *"You are an epistle of Christ"* (2 Cor. 3:3). God says this to you by the Spirit. When there is a standard that has not yet been reached in your life, God by His grace, by His mercy, and by your yieldedness can fit you for that place. You can never be prepared for it except by a broken heart and a contrite spirit, and by yielding to the will of God. But if you will come with a whole heart to the throne of grace, God will meet you and build you up on His spiritual plane.

# Nine

# How to Be Transformed

acob was on his way to the land of his fathers, but he was very troubled at the thought of meeting his brother Esau. Years before, Jacob and his mother had formed a plan to secure the blessing that Isaac was going to give Esau. How inglorious was the fulfilling of this carnal plan! It resulted in Esau's hating Jacob and saying in his heart, "When my father is dead, then will I slay my brother Jacob." (See Genesis 27:41.) Our own plans frequently lead us into disaster.

Jacob had to flee from the land, but how good the Lord was to the fugitive. He gave him a vision of a ladder and angels ascending and descending it (Gen. 28:12). How gracious is our God! He refused to have His plans of grace frustrated by the carnal workings of Jacob's mind, and that night He revealed Himself to Jacob saying, *"I am with you and will keep you wherever you go, and will bring you back to this land; for I will not leave you until I have done what I have spoken to you"* (v. 15). It is the goodness of the Lord that leads to repentance.

I believe that Jacob really did some repenting that night as he was made aware of his own meanness.

Many things may happen in our lives to show us how depraved we are by nature, but when the veil is lifted, we see how merciful and tender God is. His tender compassion is over us all the time.

From the time when Jacob had the revelation of the ladder and the angels, he had twenty-one years of testing and trial. But God had been faithful to His promise all through these years. Jacob could say to his wives, *"Your father has deceived me and changed my wages ten times, but God did not allow him to hurt me"* (Gen. 31:7). He said to his father-in-law,

> *Unless the God of my father, the God of Abra-*
> *ham and the Fear of Isaac, had been with me,*
> *surely now you would have sent me away*
> *empty-handed. God has seen my affliction and*
> *the labor of my hands.* (v. 42)

Now that Jacob was returning to the land of his birth, his heart was filled with fear. If he ever needed the Lord, it was just at this time. And he wanted to be alone with God. His wives, his children, his sheep, his cattle, his camels, and his donkeys had gone on, and *"Jacob was left alone; and a Man wrestled with him until the breaking of day"* (Gen. 32:24). The Lord saw Jacob's need and came down to meet him. It was He who wrestled with the supplanter, breaking him, changing him, transforming him.

Jacob knew that his brother Esau had power to take away all that he had, and to execute vengeance upon him. He knew that no one could deliver him but God. And there alone, lean in soul and impoverished in spirit, he met with God. Oh, how we need to get alone with God, to be broken, to be changed, to be transformed! And when we do meet with Him, He interposes, and all care and strife are brought to an end. Get alone with God, and receive the revelation of His infinite grace and of His wonderful purposes and plans for your life.

## Securing God's Blessing

This picture of Jacob left alone is so real to me, I can imagine his thoughts that night. He would think about the ladder and the angels. I somehow think that as he would begin to pray, his tongue would stick to the roof of his mouth. He knew he had to get rid of a lot of things. In days gone by, his focus had been upon himself. When we get alone with God, what a place of revelation it is! What a revelation of self we receive! And then what a revelation of the provision made for us at Calvary! It is here that we get a revelation of a life crucified with Christ, buried with Him, raised with Him, transformed by Him, and empowered by the Spirit.

Hour after hour passed. Oh, that we might spend all our nights alone with God! We are occupied too much with the things of time and this world. We need to spend time alone in the presence of God. We need to give God much time in order to receive new revelations from Him. We need to get past all the thoughts of earthly matters that crowd in so rapidly. It takes God time to deal with us. If He would only deal with us as He dealt with Jacob, then we would have power with Him, and we would prevail.

Jacob was not dry-eyed that night. Hosea tells us, *"He* [Jacob] *wept, and sought favor from Him"* (Hos. 12:4). Jacob knew that he had been a disappointment to the Lord, that he had been a groveler, but in the revelation he received that night, he saw the possibility of being transformed from a supplanter to a prince with God. The testing hour came when, at the break of day, the angel, who was none other than the Lord and Master, said, *"Let Me go, for the day breaks"* (Gen. 32:26). This is where we so often fail. Jacob knew that if God went without blessing him, Esau could not be met. You cannot meet the terrible things that await you in the world unless you secure the blessing of God.

You must never let go. Whatever you are seeking—a fresh revelation, light on the path, some particular thing—never let go. Victory is yours if you are earnest enough. If you are in darkness, if you need a fresh revelation, if your mind needs relief, if there are problems you cannot solve, lay hold of God and declare, *"I will not let You go unless You bless me!"* (v. 26).

In wrestling, the strength is in the neck, the breast, and the thigh, but the greatest strength is in the thigh. The Lord touched Jacob's thigh. With his human strength gone, surely defeat was certain. What did Jacob do? He hung on. God intends to have people who are broken. The divine power can only come when there is an end of our own self-sufficiency. But when we are broken, we must hold fast. If we let go, then we will fall short.

Jacob cried, *"I will not let You go unless You bless me!"* And God blessed him, saying, *"Your name shall no longer be called Jacob, but Israel; for you*

## How to Be Transformed

*have struggled with God and with men, and have prevailed"* (Gen. 32:28). Now a new order could begin. The old supplanter had passed away, and there was a new creation: Jacob the supplanter had been transformed into Israel the prince.

## God Is All You Need

When God comes into your life, you will find Him to be enough. As Israel came forth, the sun rose upon him, and he had power over all the things of the world and over Esau. Esau met him, but there was no fight now; there was reconciliation. They kissed each other. How true it is that *"when a man's ways please the LORD, He makes even his enemies to be at peace with him"* (Prov. 16:7). Esau inquired, "Why have you brought all these cattle, Jacob?" "Oh, that's a present," replied Jacob. "Oh, I have plenty; I don't want your cattle. What a joy to see your face again!" (See Genesis 33.) What a wonderful change! The material things did not count for much after the night of revelation. Who brought about the change? God did.

Can you hold on to God as Jacob did? You certainly can if you are sincere, if you are dependent, if you are vulnerable, if you are broken, if you are weak. It is when you are weak that you are strong (2 Cor. 12:10). But if you are self-righteous, if you are proud, if you are high-minded, if you are puffed up in your own mind, you can receive nothing from Him. If you become lukewarm instead of being on fire for God, you can become a disappointment to Him. And He says, *"I will vomit you out of My mouth"* (Rev. 3:16).

But there is a place of holiness, a place of meekness, a place of faith, where you can call to God, *"I will not let You go unless You bless me!"* (Gen. 32:26). And in response, He will bless you exceedingly abundantly above all you ask or think (Eph. 3:20).

Sometimes we are tempted to think that He has left us. Oh, no. He has promised never to leave us or forsake us (Deut. 31:6). He had promised not to leave Jacob, and He did not break His promise. He has promised not to leave us, and He will not fail. Jacob held on until the blessing came. We can do the same.

If God does not help us, we are no good for this world's need; we are no longer salt, we lose our savor. But as we spend time alone with God, and cry to Him to bless us, He re-salts us. He re-empowers us, but He brings us to brokenness and moves us into the orbit of His own perfect will.

The next morning, as the sun rose, Jacob *"limped on his hip"* (Gen. 32:31). You may ask, "What is the use of a lame man?" It is those who have seen the face of God and have been broken by Him who can meet the forces of the Enemy and break down the bulwarks of Satan's kingdom. The Word declares, *"The lame take the prey"* (Isa. 33:23). On that day, Jacob was brought to a place of dependence upon God.

Oh, the blessedness of being brought into a life of dependence upon the power of the Holy Spirit. Henceforth, we know that we are nothing without Him; we are absolutely dependent upon Him. I am absolutely nothing without the power and anointing of the Holy Spirit. Oh, for a life of absolute dependence! It is through a life of dependence that there is a life of power. If you are not there, get alone with God. If you must, spend a whole night alone with God, and let Him change and transform you. Never let Him go until He blesses you, until He makes you an Israel, a prince with God.

# Ten

# He Is Risen

od anointed Jesus, who went about doing good, for God was with Him. Today we know for a fact that He is the risen Christ. There is something about this risen, royal, glorified Christ that God means to confirm in our hearts today. The power of the risen Christ makes our hearts move and burn, and we know that there is within us that eternal working by the power of the Spirit.

Oh, beloved, it is eternal life to know Jesus! Surely the kingdom of darkness is shaken when we come into touch with that loftiness, that holiness, that divine integrity of our Master, who was so filled with power. Indeed, the grace of God was upon Him. This blessed, divine inheritance is for us. Surely God wants every one of us to catch fire. We must grasp new realities; we must cease from our murmurings; we must get into the place of triumph and exaltation.

Let's look at Acts 4:1–32. Part of this passage reads, *"And when they had prayed, the place where they were assembled together was shaken"* (v. 31). You talk about a church that cannot shout—it will never be shaken. You can write over it, "The glory has departed." It is only when men have learned the secret of the power of praying and of magnifying God that God comes forth. I have heard people say, "Oh, I praise the Lord inwardly," and nothing comes forth outwardly.

There was a man who had a large business in London. He was a great churchgoer. The church was wonderfully decorated and cushioned, and everything was comfortable enough to make him sleep. His business increased and he prospered, but he seemed to be always in a nightmare and could not tell what was bothering him.

One day he left his office to walk around the building. When he got to the door, he saw the boy who minded the door jumping and whistling. "I wish I felt like that," he said to himself. He returned to his business, but his head was in a whirl. "Oh," he said, "I will go and see the boy again." Again he went and saw the boy who was whistling and jumping. "I want to talk to you in the office," he said to the boy.

"How is it," he asked the boy, when he got into the office, "that you can always whistle and be happy?"

"I cannot help it, sir," replied the boy.

"Where did you get it?"

"I got it at the Pentecostal Mission."

"Where is that?"

And the boy told him about it. This man came to the Pentecostal church and heard about the power of God. He was broken up, and God did a wonderful thing for that man, changing him altogether. One day he was in his office, in the midst of his business, and he suddenly found himself whistling and jumping. He had changed his position.

# He Is Risen

## The Power Within

Beloved, it cannot come out of you unless it is within you. It is God who transforms the heart and life. There must be an inward working of the power of God, or it cannot come forth outwardly. We must understand that the power of Pentecost, as it came in the first order, was to loose men. People are tired of things being just smoke and deadness; they are tired of imitations. We want realities, men who have God within them, men who are always filled with God. This is a more needy day than any, and men should be filled with the Holy Spirit.

We must be like our Master. We must have definiteness about all we say. We must have all inward confidence and knowledge that we are God's property, bought and paid for by the precious blood of Jesus. Now the inheritance is in us. People may know that Jesus died and that He rose again, and yet they may not have salvation. Beloved, you must have the witness. You may know today that you are born again, for he who believes has the witness of the Spirit in him (Rom. 8:16).

It is true today that Jesus was raised up by the power of the Holy Spirit. It is true today that we in this place are risen by the power of the Spirit. It is true that we are preaching to you divine power that can raise you up, and God can set you free from all your weakness. God wants you to know how to take the victory and shout in the face of the devil and say, "Lord, it is done." (See Revelation 21:6.)

*So when they heard that, they raised their voice to God with one accord and said: "Lord,*

141

# Smith Wigglesworth on Heaven

*You are God"....And when they had prayed, the place where they were assembled together was shaken; and they were all filled with the Holy Spirit, and they spoke the word of God with boldness.* (Acts 4:24, 31)

That was a wonderful time. That was a real revival, a proper meeting. God means for us to have life. The people perceived something remarkable in the power of God changing these fishermen on the Day of Pentecost. Brothers and sisters, it is the Holy Spirit. We must not say this is merely an influence, for He is the personality and power and presence of the third person of the Trinity. Many of us have been longing for years for God to come forth, and now He is coming forth. The tide is rising everywhere. God is pouring out His Spirit in the hearts of all flesh, and they are crying before God. The day is at hand. God is fulfilling His promises.

Oh, it is lovely, the incarnation of a regeneration, a state of changing from nature to grace, from the power of Satan to God. You who are natural are made supernatural by the divine touch of Him who came to raise you from the dead. The Holy Spirit comes to abide. He comes to reveal the fullness of God. Truly, the Holy Spirit is shedding abroad in our hearts the love of God (Rom. 5:5), and He takes of the things of Jesus and shows them to us (John 16:14).

I know this great salvation that God has given us today is so large that one feels his whole body is enraptured. Do you dare leap into the power of faith right now? Do you dare take your inheritance in God? Do you dare believe God? Do you dare stand upon the record of His Word? If you will believe, you will see the glory of God (John 11:40). *"All things are possible to him who believes"* (Mark 9:23). Do you dare come near today and say that God will sanctify your body and make it holy? He wants you to have a pure body, a holy body, a separated body, a body presented on the altar of God, so that you may be no longer conformed to this world, but transformed and renewed after His image (Rom. 12:2).

## Sifted as Wheat, Tried like Gold

I believe there are people here who will be put in the place where they will have to stand upon God's Word. You will be sifted as wheat (Luke 22:31). You will be tried as though some strange thing happened to you (1 Pet. 4:12). You will be put in the most difficult places, where all hell seems to surround you, but God will sustain and empower you and will bring you into an unlimited place of faith. God will not allow you to be *"tempted beyond what you are able, but with the temptation will also make the way of escape, that you may be able to bear it"* (1 Cor. 10:13).

God will surely tell you when you have been tried sufficiently in order to bring you out as pure gold. Every trial is to prepare you for a greater position for God. Your tried faith will make you know that you will have the faith of God to go through the next trial. Who is going to live a dormant, weak, trifling, slow, indolent, prayerless, Bible-less life when he knows he must go through these things? And if you are to be made perfect in weakness, you must be tried as by fire in order to know that no man is able to win a victory unless the power of God is in him.

The Holy Spirit will lead us day by day. You will know that these light afflictions, which are only for a moment, are working out for us an eternal weight of glory (2 Cor. 4:17).

Oh, beloved, what are we going to do with this day? We must have a high tide this afternoon. We must have people receive the Holy Spirit; we must have people healed in their seats; we must see God come forth. Some of you have been longing for the Holy Spirit. God can baptize you just where you are. There may be some here who have not yet tasted of the grace of God. Close beside you is the water of life. Have a drink, brother, sister, for God says, *"And let him who thirsts come. Whoever desires, let him take the water of life freely"* (Rev. 22:17). *"If we love one another, God abides in us, and His love has been perfected in us"* (1 John 4:12).

Eleven

# Rising into the Heavenlies

 want to read to you a few verses from 1 Peter 1. I believe that God wants to speak to us to strengthen our position in faith and grace. Beloved, I want you to understand that you will get more than you came for. There is not a person in this place who will get what he came for, because God always gives more. No man gets his answers to his prayers—he never does—for God answers his prayers abundantly above what he asks or thinks.

Don't say, "I got nothing." You got as much as you came for, and more. But if your minds are not willing to be yielded, and your hearts are not sufficiently consecrated, you will find that you are limited on that line, because the heart is the place of reception. God wants you to have receptive hearts that will take in the mind of God. These wonderful Scriptures are full of life-giving power. Let us read the first and second verses. There are some words that I ought to lay emphasis on.

*Peter, an apostle of Jesus Christ, to the pilgrims of the Dispersion in Pontus, Galatia,*

145

# Smith Wigglesworth on Heaven

*Cappadocia, Asia, and Bithynia, elect according to the foreknowledge of God the Father, in sanctification of the Spirit, for obedience and sprinkling of the blood of Jesus Christ: Grace to you and peace be multiplied.* (1 Pet. 1:1–2)

I want you to notice that in all times, in all histories of the world, whenever there has been a divine rising or revelation, God coming forth with new dispensational orders of the Spirit, you will find there have been persecutions all over. Take the case of the three Hebrew children, Shadrach, Meshach, and Abednego, and also Daniel and Jeremiah. With any person in the old dispensation, as much as in the new, when the Spirit of the Lord has been moving mightily, there has arisen trouble and difficulty. Why? Because of things that are very much against revelations of God and the Spirit of God.

## Elected by God

Humanity, flesh, and natural things are all against divine things. Evil powers work upon this position of the human life, especially when the will is unyielded to God. Then, the powers of darkness rise up against the powers of divine order, but they never defeat them. Divine order is very often in the minority, but always in the majority. Did I say that right? Yes, and I meant it, too. Wickedness may increase and abound, but when the Lord raises His flag over the saint, it is victory. Though it is in the minority, it always triumphs.

I want you to notice the first verse because it says *"Dispersion."* This was meant to say that these people did not have much liberty to meet together, so they were driven from place to place. Even in the days of the Scottish religious reformer John Knox, the people who served God had to be in very close quarters, because the Roman church set out to destroy them, nailed them to judgment seats, and destroyed them in all sorts of ways. They were in the minority, but they swept through in victory, and the Roman power was crushed and defeated. Take care that such a thing does not rise again. May God bring us into such perfect order that we may understand these days, that we may be in the minority, but we will always obtain the victory through God.

The Holy Spirit wants us to understand our privileges: we are *"elect according to the foreknowledge of God...in sanctification of the Spirit"* (1 Pet. 1:2). Now this sanctification of the Spirit is not on the lines of being cleansed from sin. It is a higher order than the work of redemption. The blood of Jesus is rich unto all powerful cleansing, and it takes away other powers and transforms us by the mighty power of God. But when sin is gone, yes, when we are clean and when we know we have the Word of God right in us and the power of the Spirit is bringing everything to a place where we triumph, then comes revelation by the power of the Spirit, lifting us onto higher ground, into all the fullness of God, which unveils Christ in such a way.

This is what is called sanctification of the Spirit: sanctified by the Spirit, elect according to the foreknowledge of God. I don't want you to stumble at the word *elect*—it is a most blessed word. You might say you are all elect: everyone in this place could say he is one of the elect. God has designed that all men should be saved. This is the election, but whether you accept and come into your election, whether you prove yourself worthy of your election, whether you have so allowed the Spirit to fortify you, whether you have done this I don't know, but your election, your sanctification, is to be seated at the right hand of God.

This word *election* is a very precious word to me. Foreordained, predestined—these are words that God designed before the world was, to bring us into triumph and victory in Christ. Some people play around with it and make it a goal. They say, "Oh, well, you see, we are elected, we are all right." I know many of them who believe in that condition of election, and they say they are quite all right because they are elected to be saved. I believe these people are so diplomatic that they believe others can be elected to be damned. It is not true! Everybody is elected to be saved, but whether they come into it, that is another thing.

Many don't come into salvation because the god of this world has blinded their eyes *"lest the light of the gospel of the glory...should shine on them"* (2 Cor. 4:4). What does that mean? It means that Satan has mastery over their minds, and they have an ear to listen to corrupt things. Be careful of things that do not have Jesus in them. I sometimes shout for all I am worth about Jesus, because I know there is no Jesus inside some things.

Beloved, I want you to see this election I am speaking about, to catch a glimpse of heaven, with your heart always on the wing, where you grasp everything spiritual, when everything divine makes you hungry for it.

# Rising into the Heavenlies

If I returned to this place in a year's time, I would see this kind of election gone right forward, always full, never having a bad report, where you see Christ in some vision, in some way in your lives every day, growing in the knowledge of God every day. But I cannot dwell there, for we have much to get through. It is through the sanctification of the Spirit unto obedience and the sprinkling of the blood of Jesus Christ. There is no sanctification if it is not sanctification unto obedience.

## Obedient to the Word

There would be no trouble with any of us if we would come definitely to a place where we understood these words of Jesus: *"And for their sakes I sanctify Myself, that they also may be sanctified by the truth"* (John 17:19). *"Sanctify them by Your truth. Your word is truth"* (v. 17).

No child of God ever asks a question about the Word of God. What do I mean? The Word of God is clear on the breaking of bread, the Word of God is clear on water baptism, the Word of God is clear on all these things, and no person who was going on to the obedience and sanctification of the Spirit by election would pray questioningly over that Word. The Word of God is to be swallowed, not prayed over.

If ever you pray over the Word of God, there is some disobedience; you are not willing to obey. If you come into obedience on the Word of God, and it says anything about water baptism, you will obey. If it says anything about speaking in tongues, you will obey. If it says anything about the breaking of bread and the assembling of ourselves together, you will

149

obey. If you come into the election of the sanctification of the Spirit, you will be obedient in everything revealed in that Word. And to the degree that you are not obedient, you have not come into the sanctification of the Spirit.

A little thing spoils many good things. (See Ecclesiastes 10:1.) People say, "Mr. So-and-so is very good, but…." Or, "Mrs. So-and-so is excellent, but…." "Oh, you know that young man is progressing tremendously, but…."

There are no *but*s in the sanctification of the Spirit. *But* and *if* are gone, and it is *shall* and *I will* all the way through.

Beloved, if there are any *but*s in your attitude toward the Word of truth, there is something unyielded to the Spirit. I pray to God the Holy Spirit that we may be willing to yield ourselves to the sanctification of the Spirit, that we may be in the mind of God in the election, that we may have the mind of God in the possession of it. Perhaps to encourage you, it would be helpful to show you what election is, because there is no difficulty in proving whether you are elected or not.

## The Spirit Moves upon You

If you, as a believer, searched your own heart as to why you have been attending these meetings, perhaps you would not have to say, "Because it was Wigglesworth." That would be a mistake. But if there was in you that holy calling—that strange, inward, longing desire for more of God—you could say it was the sanctification of the Spirit that was drawing you. Who could do that except He who has elected you for that?

# Rising into the Heavenlies

It does not matter what age you are. If I were to say to you, "Stand up, you who never remember the time when the Spirit did not strive with you," it would be a marvelous thing how many people would stand. What do you call it? God bringing you in, moving upon you. Strange? Very strange!

When I think of my own case, I recall that on my mother's side and on my father's side there was no desire for God, and yet in my very infancy I was strangely moved upon by the Spirit. At the age of eight years, I was definitely saved, and at nine years I felt the Spirit come upon me, just as when I spoke in tongues. I was *"elect according to the foreknowledge of God"* (1 Pet. 1:2), and there are people in this place who have had the same experience. You might say, "When I was in sin, I was troubled." And there is a direct line of election between God and the human man, moving it, being wholly prepared for God.

It is a most blessed thought that we have a God of love, compassion, and grace, who does not will the death of even one sinner. God has made it possible for all men to be saved by causing Jesus, His well-beloved Son, to die for the sins of all people. It is true that He took our sins; it is true that He paid the price for the whole world; it is true that He gave Himself as a ransom for many; it is true, beloved. And you say, "For whom?" *"Whoever desires, let him take the water of life freely"* (Rev. 22:17).

"What about the others?" you ask. It would be a direct refusal of the blood of Jesus; it would have to be a refusal to have Christ to reign over them, that's it. It is *"whoever desires"* on this side and whoever does not on the other side. There are people living in the world who do not desire this. What is up with them? *"The god of this age has blinded* [them], *who do not believe, lest the light of the gospel of the glory of Christ, who is the image of God, should shine on them"* (2 Cor. 4:4).

### Peace and Hope

*Elect according to the foreknowledge of God the Father, in sanctification of the Spirit, for obedience and sprinkling of the blood of Jesus Christ: Grace to you and peace be multiplied.*
                                        (1 Pet. 1:2)

Through sanctification of the Spirit, according to the election, you will get to a place where you are not disturbed. There is a peace in sanctification of the Spirit, because it is a place of revelation, taking you into heavenly places. It is a place where God comes and speaks and makes Himself known to you, and when you are face-to-face with God, you get a peace *"which surpasses all understanding"* (Phil. 4:7), lifting you from state to state of inexpressible wonderment. It is really wonderful.

> Oh, this is like heaven to me,
> This is like heaven to me,
> I've stepped over Jordan to Canaan's fair land;
> And this is like heaven to me.

Oh, it is wonderful!

*Blessed be the God and Father of our Lord Jesus Christ, who according to His abundant mercy has begotten us again to a living hope through the resurrection of Jesus Christ from the dead.* (1 Pet. 1:3)

# Rising into the Heavenlies

We cannot pass that up, because this sanctification of the Spirit brings us into definite alignment with this wonderful hope of the glory of God. I want to keep before us the glory, the joy of this lively hope. A lively hope is opposite of a dead hope, exactly opposite to normal.

Lively hope is movement. Lively hope is looking into. Lively hope is pressing into. Lively hope is leaving everything behind you. Lively hope is keeping the vision. Lively hope sees Him coming! And you live in it—the lively hope. You are not trying to make yourself feel that you are believing, but the lively hope is ready and waiting. Lively hope is filled with joy of expectation of the King. Praise the Lord!

I want you to know that God has this in His mind for you. Do you know what will move them? The real joy in expectation that will come forth with manifestation and then realization. Don't you know?

Well, I pray God the Holy Spirit that He will move you that way. Come now, beloved, I want to raise your hopes into such activity, into such a joyful experience, that when you go away from this meeting you will have such joy that you would walk if you could not run, that you would jump in a car if you could not run, and that you would go at full speed if you knew you could be there any faster.

Now, I trust that you will be so reconciled to God that there is not one thing that would interfere with your having this lively hope. If you had any love for the world, it could not be, for Jesus is not coming to the world. Jesus is coming to the heavenlies, and all the heavenlies are going to Him, so you cannot have anything but joy with it. You could not have the pride of life. All these things are contrary to the lively hope because of the greatness and the magnificent, multitudinous glories of the regions of eternity, which are placed before you in joyful expectation.

### Interpretation of Tongues

The joy of the Lord is everything. The soul lifts up like the golden grain ready to be gathered in for the great sheaf. All ready, waiting, rejoicing, longing for Him, until they say, "Lord Jesus, we cannot wait any longer."

What a wonderful expression of the Holy Spirit to the soul in interpretation. How He loves us, hovers over us, rejoices in us! How the Lord by the Holy Spirit takes a great drink with us, and our cup is full and running over (Ps. 23:5)!

*"The joy of the LORD is your strength"* (Neh. 8:10). You have to be right in these glorious places, for it is the purpose of God for your soul. I hope you won't forget the lively hope. Do not live for tomorrow because you did not catch it today. Oh, it is wonderful. Hallelujah!

### Our Inheritance as His Children

*"To an inheritance incorruptible and undefiled and that does not fade away, reserved in heaven for you"* (1 Pet. 1:4).

First, incorruptible. Second, undefiled. Third, does not fade away. Fourth, reserved in heaven for you. Glory to God! I tell you, it is great, it is very great. May the Lord help you to thirst after this glorious life of Jesus. Oh, brother, it is more than new wine; the Holy Spirit is more than new wine; the

# Rising into the Heavenlies

Holy Spirit is the manifestation of the glories of the new creation.

This is an incorruptible inheritance. *Incorruptible* is one of those delightful words that God wants all believers to grasp. Everything corruptible fades away; everything seen cannot remain. Jesus said, *"Where neither moth nor rust destroys and where thieves do not break in and steal"* (Matt. 6:20). None of these things are joined up with incorruptible. Incorruptible is what is eternal, everlasting, divine. Therefore, everything spiritual and divine reaches a place where God truly is—what shall I say?—where God truly is in the midst of it. He is in existence from everlasting to everlasting: holy, pure, divine, incorruptible.

This is one part of our inheritance in the Spirit, only one part. Hallelujah! It is an inheritance incorruptible and undefiled. Oh, how beautiful it is, perfected forever, no spot, no wrinkle, holy, absolutely pure, all traces of sin withered. Everything that is mortal has been scattered and has come into a place so purified that God is in the midst of it. Hallelujah! It is so lovely to think of that great and wonderful city we read about in Revelation: *"Then I, John, saw the holy city, New Jerusalem, coming down out of heaven from God, prepared as a bride adorned for her husband"* (Rev. 21:2).

Think about it, the Marriage. Oh, it is glorious. "I saw the holy city *'as a bride adorned for her husband,'*" undefiled, glorious, all white, all pure. Who were the people who are now the bride of Christ? They were once in the world, once corruptible, once defiled, but now they have been made holy and spiritual by the blood. They are now lifted from

155

corruptible to incorruptible and are now undefiled in the presence of God. Hallelujah!

Oh, beloved, God intends this for us today. Every soul in this place must reach out to this ideal perfection. God has ten thousand more thoughts for you than you have for yourself. The grace of God is going to move us on, and you will never sorrow anymore as long as you live. You will never weep anymore, but you will weep for joy.

This inheritance is undefiled; it does not fade away. It does not fade away! What a heaven of bliss, what a joy of delight, what a foretaste of heaven on earth. Everything earthly will fade away in the splendor of that glorious day; it all withers when you get in the Spirit. You would cheerfully do the work you have to do because of tomorrow in the presence of the King. Oh, brother, what a hope, what a joyous possibility, within a short time to be in that mighty multitude.

But you say, "My burden is more than I can bear." Cheerfully bear the burden, for tomorrow you will be there. No sin will entice you, no evil spirit will be able to trip you, no, because tomorrow you will be with the Lord. With the Lord forever, an inheritance that does not fade away.

Now let us go on a little further. *"Who are kept by the power of God through faith for salvation ready to be revealed in the last time"* (1 Pet. 1:5). I would like to say something along the lines of salvation, because salvation is very much misunderstood. Salvation that comes to you in a moment of time, believing unto salvation, is only the beginning. Salvation is so tremendous, mighty, and wonderful, as the early apostles said: "Being saved every day." You begin with God and go right on to being saved day by day (2 Cor. 4:16). *"Forgetting those things which are behind and reaching forward"* (Phil. 3:13), through the power of the blood you go on unto salvation.

Salvation is like sanctification of the Spirit; it is not a goal, no. It is only a goal when you limit yourself. There is no limitation as we see the great preservation of the Master. We should never stand still for a moment, but we should mightily move on in God.

## Rejoice in Being Purified

*"In this you greatly rejoice, though now for a little while, if need be, you have been grieved by various trials"* (1 Pet. 1:6). Ah, what a blessing, you have no idea what God will mean to you in trials and temptations—it is purification of the Spirit.

> *That the genuineness of your faith, being much more precious than gold that perishes, though it is tested by fire, may be found to praise, honor, and glory at the revelation of Jesus Christ.* (1 Pet. 1:7)

Gold perishes, but faith never perishes; it is more precious than gold, although it may be tried with fire. I went into a place one day, and a gentleman said to me, "Would you like to see the purification of gold this morning?" I replied, "Yes." He got some gold and put it in a crucible and put a blast of heat on it. First, it became bloodred, and then it changed and changed. Then this man took an instrument and passed it over the gold, drawing something off that was foreign to the gold. He did this several times until every part was taken away, and then at last he put it over again and said, "Look," and there we both saw our faces in the gold. It was wonderful.

Dear believer, the trial of your faith is much more precious than gold that perishes. When God so purifies you through trials, misunderstandings, persecution, and suffering because you are wrongfully judged, because you have not believed what people say to you, Jesus has given you the keynote: rejoice in that day.

Beloved, as you are tested in the fire, the Master is cleaning away everything that cannot bring out the image of Him in you. He is cleaning away all the dross from your life, and every evil power, until He sees His face right in the life, until He sees His face right in your life.

*"Always carrying about in the body the dying of the Lord Jesus, that the life of Jesus also may be manifested in our body"* (2 Cor. 4:10). It may not seem to any of us to be very joyous, because it is not acceptable to the flesh, but I have told you already that your flesh is against the Spirit. Your flesh and all your human powers have to be perfectly submitted to the mighty power of God inwardly, to express and manifest His glory outwardly. But you must be willing for the process and say "Amen" to God. It may be very hard, but God will help you.

It is lovely to know that in the chastening times, in the times of misunderstanding and hard tests when you are in the right and are treated as though you were in the wrong, God is meeting you and blessing you. People say it is the devil. Never mind, let the fire burn; it will do you good. Don't begin complaining, but endure it joyfully. It is so sweet to understand this: *"Love suffers long and is kind"* (1 Cor. 13:4). How lovely to get to a place where you think no evil, you are not easily provoked, and you can bear all things and endure all things! Praise the Lord. Oh, the glory of it, the joy of it!

I understand what it means to jump for joy. I could jump for joy this morning. Why? Because of the Lord.

> I know the Lord, I know the Lord,
> I know the Lord has laid His hand on me.

*"Whom having not seen you love. Though now you do not see Him, yet believing, you rejoice with joy inexpressible and full of glory"* (1 Pet. 1:8). We love our Lord Jesus Christ, whom we have not seen. Oh, how sweet, there is no voice so gentle, so soft, so full of tenderness to me. There is no voice like His, and there is no touch like His. Is it possible to love the One we have not seen? God will make it possible to all. *"Though now you do not see Him, yet believing, you rejoice with joy inexpressible and full of glory."*

## Submitted to the Lord

Rejoice? Oh, what a salvation God has procured for us, and yet we are nothing; we are worthless and helpless in ourselves. I entreat you from the Lord to be so reconciled to Him that there will be no division between you and Him. When He laughs you will laugh, and when He sees you in tears His compassion will be all you need forever. Will you give Him preference? Will you give Him preeminence in all things? Should He not have His right place and decide for you the way and plan of your life?

Believer, when you allow Him to decide for you, when you want nothing but His blessed will, when He is Lord and Governor over all, heaven will be there all the time. The Lord bless you with grace today to leave all and say, "I will follow You, Lord Jesus."

All of you who are longing to get nearer Jesus this morning, I ask you in the name of Jesus to surrender yourselves to Him. But you say, "Wigglesworth, I did it yesterday." I know, but this morning you need to do it more. I know I want to get nearer to my Lord. Let us rise and get near to Him for a few minutes.

Twelve

# Preparation for
# the Rapture

ur hearts are moved. God is moving us to believe that He is on the throne waiting for us to make application. Stretch out your hands to God to believe that the almightiness of His grace is for us in a most marvelous way. Whatever yesterday was, today is to be greater.

Are you ready? What for? To come to a place where you will not give way, where you will dare believe that God is the same today and will surely make you satisfied because He longs to fill you. Those who believe will be satisfied.

Are you ready? What for? That you may so apply your heart to the will of God, so yield yourself to His purposes, that God will have a plan through your life that never before has been.

Are you ready? What for? That today you may so come into like-mindedness with Christ, that you may have no more human desire but will be cut short from all human bondages and set free. The shoreline must never know you more. Come to God in all His fullness, His revelation, His power, that you may be clothed upon with God today.

# Smith Wigglesworth on Heaven

I believe you all believe in the coming of the Lord and the Rapture that is to take place. I am going to deal with what will take you right up to the Rapture. To this end, read the fifth chapter of 2 Corinthians.

This is one of those divine propositions. It is one of those openings to the heart of enlarged ideas. It is one of those moments when we enter in by faith to see that we can be so occupied, so changed, so in Christ, so ready, so clothed upon, and so filled with Him until the very breath of the life of what is causing it would cause us to leave this place.

Do not allow your natural inclinations to interfere with supernatural evidences. You never will be what God has ordered you to be until you are willing to denounce your own failings, your unbelief, and all human standards. You must be willing to denounce them so that you might stand in place, complete, believing that you are a new creation in the Spirit. In a mighty way, God can so fill you with life and can destroy all that is natural that would interfere with the process of change until you are made alive unto God by the Spirit, ready for the Lord's coming.

## A Higher Plane

Here we have a definite position. Paul had a great deal of revelation. In fact, Peter said that Paul said many things that are hard to understand. "Nevertheless," he said, "we know they are of the Lord." (See 2 Peter 3:15–18.) Paul had many hard things to see. Unless we are spiritually enlightened, we will not be able to comprehend the attitude of the place of ascension he had reached.

# Preparation for the Rapture

All your spiritual acquaintances must come into ascension. Always keep in mind that to be conformed to this world is all loss, but to be transformed from this world is all gain. And the transforming is the working in of His mighty power in the mind.

The body and the soul can be so preserved in this wonderful life of God until there is not one thing that could hinder us. We are dead to sin, alive unto God. Sin is destroyed, disease is absolutely put outside, and death is abolished in the life of the resurrection of Christ in the body.

The Spirit of the Lord is giving us revelation that will teach us a plane that is so supernatural in the human realm that you will live absolutely in a new creation if you dare to believe. You will go by leaps and bounds into all the treasury of the Most High as you believe.

Nothing will interfere with you but yourself, and I believe God can change even your mind. He can give you much aspiration and inflate you with holiness, with life from Himself. He will fill you with great ambition for purity, holiness, and transformation, which means that you will be transported toward heaven.

God has to cause revolution many times in the body before He can get the throne. He causes you to come to death, and then to death, and then to death. He will cause you to see that sin violates, that it hinders progress, and He will show you that anything of the natural is not divine. He will teach you that you have to have the divine mind; you have to have a new mind, a new will. He will show you that everything about you must be in the line of consecration, separated entirely unto perfection.

Believe it. Perhaps, as you examine yourself, you will think that it never could be. Get your mind off yourself; that is destruction. Get your mind on the Lord.

No building could be built without a plumb line and a straight edge. The Word of God is a true plumb line. God has given us a plumb line and a straight edge, causing us to be built in supernatural lines so that we may be an edifice in the Spirit. He causes us to be strong against the devil.

### Interpretation of Tongues

Weakness may be turned into power, feeblemindedness into the mind of Christ. The whole body fitly joined together in the Spirit can rise and rise, until it is an edifice in the Holy Spirit. It is not what it is; it is what it is going to be. God has made preparation for us to be freed from the law of sin and death. He has gained the victory. He has overcome and vanquished the Enemy, and the last enemy that will be destroyed is death (1 Cor. 15:26).

Yes, deeper, deeper, higher, higher, holier, purer, purer, until God sets His seal upon us; we are His forever, bought with a price, not with silver and gold, but with the precious blood.

Let the Spirit move you, chasten you, bring you to nothing, because you must be so chastened by the Lord in order to have the fruits of His holiness. He compares you this morning to that position of fruitfulness. Unless you die, you cannot live. So, in the very attitude of death, He causes resurrection force to come into your life, until you come out of all things into the living Head; until Christ is over you, nourishing you in the mind, in the body, and causing your spirit to live until you feel the very breath of heaven breathing upon you and the wings of the Spirit moving within you.

## Getting Ready for the Future Exit

*For we know that if our earthly house, this tent, is destroyed, we have a building from God, a house not made with hands, eternal in the heavens. For in this we groan, earnestly desiring to be clothed with our habitation which is from heaven.* (2 Cor. 5:1–2)

This verse speaks about a present tense that has to make us ready for a future exit. Present-tense lessons are wonderful. You miss a great deal if you do not live in the present tense. You must never put anything off until tomorrow. "Remember today if you will believe."

The Word of God says, *"The same yesterday, today, and forever"* (Heb. 13:8). God wants us to have everything today. Don't say, "Tomorrow I will be healed." Don't say, "Tomorrow I will be baptized." Don't say, "Tomorrow I will have more light." Today, if you will hear His voice, do not harden your heart, for the hearing of faith is wonderful.

Two things are real that must take place, but it is our responsibility to be in readiness for these things to take place. We should all wish that no one would die from this day forward. Whenever the Scriptures speak of death, it is *"sown in dishonor"* (1 Cor. 15:43). We know God is going to raise in power.

## Smith Wigglesworth on Heaven

However, there is a state in which we may go on to see that sin, disease, and death are destroyed, that we have come into a plan of such an enforcement of resurrection power that we need not die if we dare believe the truth. But we are on the edge and frightened all the time that it won't come to pass.

### Surpassing Joy

I want to help you today. If you are not moved in some way, God is not with you. One of two things has to happen: either you have to be moved so that you cannot rest, or you have to be made so glad that you cannot remain in the same place. I could not believe that anybody filled with the Spirit could speak to an assembly of people, and they would still be the same after he had finished. So I take it for granted that God has me here to move you, to make you very thirsty, or to cause a gladness to come into your heart that will absolutely surpass everything else along the lines of joy.

### The Body Must Be Changed

No flesh can come into the presence of God. If no flesh can come into the presence of God, then what is going into the presence of God? If you do die, the process is to get rid of all that there is in the body. The very body that you are in must be disposed of. If it goes away, it must come to ashes. There is no such thing as your body being in the presence of God. So your body has to give place to a resurrection order, to a resurrection life. It has to.

The Scriptures speak about dissolving. If your body does not go through the process of death—if it does not experience just what earthly cabbages, potatoes, corn, and wheat experience—if it does not go that way and get rid of all its acquaintances, then God will cause the old body to be turned into gases when it goes up. There will not be a bit of it left. But the very nature of Christ, the life of God, the very essence of life, in that moment, will be clothed upon with a body that can stand all eternity.

So be ready for a change. You say, "How can we be ready?" I will explain. Follow me very closely.

*"In this we groan"* (2 Cor. 5:2). There should be a groaning attitude, a place where we see that there is some defect, that there is not perfect purification going on. When we come to that attitude, knowing we are bound in the way, then we will groan to be delivered.

What is the deliverance? Will it be in this present world? Certainly. I am not in heaven yet; I am on the earth. I am dealing with people who are in the earth, who can be in the earth and have this supernatural abounding within them. Now let us see how this can be.

*"Having been clothed, we shall not be found naked"* (v. 3). I am dealing with clothing now. The first time the body was clothed with flesh; this time it is being clothed with the Spirit.

The very nature that came into you when you were born again was a spiritual quality of knowledge. It understands supernatural things. It has power to compare spiritual things with spiritual things, and only those who are born of God can understand spiritual things. The world that has never been saved cannot understand them. But the moment we are quickened, born again, and made anew, this nature will take its supernatural powers and will go on travailing and groaning to be delivered from the body. And it will go on crying and crying until the saints are seen in large numbers saying, *"Come, Lord Jesus!"* (Rev. 22:20), and the consummation will be most remarkable.

But I believe God has a plan for us even before that may happen. Carefully, thoughtfully read the fourth verse of 2 Corinthians 5: *"For we who are in this tent groan, being burdened, not because we want to be unclothed, but further clothed, that mortality may be swallowed up by life."*

*"Further clothed."* We do not desire to go, but to stop, because we realize we are not exactly ready to go. But we want to be so clothed with the Spirit while we are in the body, clothed with the life from heaven, that not one natural thing will be evident. We are then absolutely made alive in Christ, and we live only for the glory and the exhibition of the Lord of life.

Paul said that nothing good dwelled in his flesh (Rom. 7:18). You know exactly what nakedness is. They knew, when Jesus walked the earth, that their nakedness was made bare. You know that nakedness is a sense of consciousness that there is something that has not been dealt with, has not been judged, and the blood has not had its perfect application. Nakedness means that you are inwardly conscious that there is some hidden thing, something that has not been absolutely brought to the blood, something that could not stand God, something that is not ready for the absolute glory of God.

Then there is the principle of life. I want to speak about the life of the Word of Life itself. The

# Preparation for the Rapture

Word of Life is preached to you through the Gospel, and it has a wonderful power in it. It deals with the natural realm and brings immortality into the natural, until the natural realizes the first spring of supernatural power in the heart. From that moment, a man knows he is in the earth but belongs to heaven, and this life that is in him is a life that has the power to eat up mortality. A couple of verses from Romans will help us here:

> There is therefore now no condemnation to those who are in Christ Jesus, who do not walk according to the flesh, but according to the Spirit. For the law of the Spirit of life....
>
> (Rom. 8:1–2)

The law of life is the law that came into you that is incorruptible, that is divine, that is the nature of the Son of God.

Suppose I were dealing with the coming of the Lord. The revelation that I have about the Lord's return is that all those who are going to be caught up are going to be eaten up—their old natures, their old desires, their old lives are going to be eaten up with His life, so that when He comes His life will meet the life that is in them. But the process we are going through now is to build us on the lines of readiness.

## The Life That Eats Mortality

Now I want to speak of the life that has power to eat up mortality. What is mortality? When I speak about mortality, you no doubt think of your physical body and say, "That is mortality."

That is not mortality. That is not what will be swallowed up or eaten up. As long as you are in the world, you will want the casket that your body truly is. But it is what is in the body that is mortal that has to be eaten up with immortality.

If I were to go through Mark, Luke, Romans, Galatians, Timothy, and Peter, I would find sixty-six different descriptions of mortality. I would find sedition, heresy, envy, strife, malice, hatred, murder, emulation, witchcraft. I would find covetousness, adultery, fornication. I would discover that all these were mortality. But I would also find a life in the supernatural that can eat them up, devour them, and destroy them until there is no condemnation in this body.

The Scriptures are very clear that we must allow ourselves to come into touch with this great Life in us, this wonderful Life divine, this Christ form, this spiritual revelation.

Do not forget that the Holy Spirit did not come as a cleanser. The Holy Spirit is not a cleanser; the Holy Spirit is a revealer of imperfection that can only be cleansed by the blood of Jesus. After the blood has cleansed you, you need the Word of God, for the Word of God is the only power that creates anew. Life comes through the Word. The Word is the Son; the Word is the life of the Son. He who has received the Son has received life; he who has not received the Son has not received life (John 3:36).

There are millions of people living today who do not have life. There is only one life that is eternal, and that is the life of the Son of God. One is a life of death, eternal death; the other is a life of eternal life. One is destruction; the other is eternal deliverance.

One is bondage; the other is freedom. One is sorrow; the other is joy.

I want you to see that you are to live so full of this divine life, until you are not moved by any *"wind of doctrine"* (Eph. 4:14), or anything else that comes along.

People make the biggest mistake in the world, and they miss the greatest things today, because they turn to the letter instead of the Spirit. How many people have been ruined because they have gone mad on water baptism? You cannot prove to me through any part of Scripture that baptism can save you. It is only a form. And yet, people are mad and are firm in their belief that if you are not baptized, you must be lost. These people understand only the letter, and the letter always kills. The Spirit always gives life.

The person, whoever he is, who would turn you from the baptism of Matthew 28 to any other baptism, is a thief and a robber and is trying to destroy you. Do not be carnally minded. Be spiritually minded; then you will know the truth, and the truth will make you free (John 8:32).

See to it that you live and affirm and know that it is Christ who gives life. Division brings sorrow, remorse, trials, and difficulties. Let Christ dwell in your hearts richly by faith.

Don't go mad on preaching only the baptism of the Holy Spirit; you will be lopsided. Don't go mad on preaching water baptism; you will be lopsided. Don't go mad on preaching healing; you will be lopsided. There is only one thing that you will never become lopsided over, and that is preaching salvation. The only power is the Gospel of the kingdom.

Men are not saved by baptism, not even by the baptism of the Holy Spirit, or by the baptism in water. They are saved and preserved by the blood of Christ.

The Lord wants to bring us to the place of real foundation truth. Build upon the foundation truth. Don't be twisted aside by anything. Let this be your chief motive: that you are living to catch more of the Spirit, and only the Spirit.

I clearly know that the Holy Spirit is not the only means of making me eligible for the coming of the Lord. Lots of people have gone mad because they have gotten baptized with the Spirit and think no one is right but those who are baptized with the Spirit. It is the biggest foolishness in the world. Why is it foolishness? Because the truth bears it out all the time. The thief on the cross went right up to meet Jesus in paradise. But just because a thief missed these things, will we miss them, too? No. It was the great grace and mercy of the Lord to have mercy upon him. There is not a gift, not a grace, not a position except those that God uses to loosen you from your bondages, and He wants you to be free in the Spirit. He wants to fill you with the Holy Spirit, wants to fill you with the Word, until He brings you to the place of the sealing of the Spirit.

You say, "What is the sealing of the Spirit?" The sealing of the Spirit is that God has put His mark upon you and you are tagged. It is a wonderful thing to have the tag of the Almighty. It seals you. The devil cannot touch you. The Lord has preserved you. There is a covenant between you and God, and the sealing of the Spirit has got you to the place where evil powers have no more dominion.

## Preparation for the Rapture

Don't go away with the idea that I am preaching a perfection in which you cannot sin. There is a place of perfection, of purifying as He is pure, so that we cannot commit sins. There is no man who can commit sin if he is being purified. But it is when he ceases from seeking deeper experience, a holier vocation, a deeper separation, a perfect place where he and Christ are one, that sin comes in. Only in Christ is there security.

Let no man think that he cannot fall because he stands. No, but let us remember this: we need not fall. Grace abounds where sin abounds, and where weakness is, grace comes in. Your very inactivity becomes divine activity. Where absolute weakness is so strong that you feel you cannot stand the trial, He comes in and enables you to stand. Life is ministered, and Christ takes the place of weakness, for *"when I am weak, then am I strong"* (2 Cor. 12:10), for then God touches me with His strength.

This is ideal. This is divine appointment. This is holy installation. This is God's thought from the throne. The Lord is speaking to us, and I would say with a trumpet voice through to the whole world, "Be holy!" Don't fail to see that God wants you ready for translation. Holiness is the habitation of God.

### Spiritual Drunkenness

There is a place to reach in the Holy Spirit that is mystifying to the world and to many people who are not going on with God. Here is a most remarkable lesson. We can be so filled with the Spirit, so clothed upon by Him, so purified within, so made ready for the Rapture, that all the time we are drunk. *"For if we are beside ourselves, it is for God; or if we are of sound mind, it is for you"* (2 Cor. 5:13).

You can be so filled with the Spirit of life that you are absolutely drunken and beside yourself. Now, when I come in contact with people who would criticize my drunkenness, I am sober. I can be sober one minute; I can be drunk the next. I tell you, to be drunk is wonderful! *"And do not be drunk with wine, in which is dissipation; but be filled with the Spirit"* (Eph. 5:18). In this there is a lively hope, filled with indiscreetness in regard to what anyone else thinks.

Think of a man who is drunk. He stops at a lamppost, and he has a lot to say to it. He says the most foolish things possible, and the people say, "He's gone."

Oh, Lord, that I may be so drunk with You that it makes no difference what people think! I am not concerned with what people think. I am speaking to the Lord in hymns and spiritual songs, making my boast in the Lord. The Lord of Hosts is around me, and I am so free in the Holy Spirit that I am ready to be taken to heaven. But He does not take me. Why doesn't He take me? I am ready, and it is better for me to go, but for the church's sake it is preferable that I stop. (See Philippians 1:23–25.)

It is best that I am clothed upon with the Spirit, living in the midst of the people, showing no nakedness. I need to be full of purity, full of power, full of revelation for the church's sake. It is far better to go, but for the church's sake I must stop, so that I may be helpful, telling the people how they can have their nakedness covered, how all their imperfections can be covered, how all the mind can be clothed, how all their inward impurities are made pure in the presence of God. It is better that I am living, walking, and acting in the Holy Spirit. This may seem impossible, yet this is the height that God wants us to reach.

Here is another verse to help you. It is a keynote verse to many positions I am teaching here. *"And if Christ is in you, the body is dead because of sin, but the Spirit is life because of righteousness"* (Rom. 8:10). There is no such thing as having liberty in your body if there is any sin there. When righteousness is there, righteousness abounds. When Christ is in your heart, enthroning your life, and sin is dethroned, then righteousness abounds and the Holy Spirit has great liberty. This is one of the highest positions of the Scripture character.

*"And if children, then heirs; heirs of God and joint heirs with Christ"* (v. 17). My, what triumphs of heights, of lengths, of depths, of breadths there are in this holy place! Where is it? Right inside.

### Interpretation of Tongues

He who is dead is free from sin (Rom. 6:7) but is alive unto God by the Spirit, and is made free from the law of sin and death (Rom. 8:2). He has entered into a relationship in God, and now God is his reward. He is not only a son, but he is also joined in heirship, because of sonship. In purity, he is joined together with Him, and He will withhold no good thing from him who walks uprightly (Ps. 84:11). Every good thing is for us on the holy line, walking uprightly, being set free, being made God's property.

# Smith Wigglesworth on Heaven

## Reconciliation in Christ

*"All things are of God, who has reconciled us to Himself through Jesus Christ, and has given us the ministry of reconciliation"* (2 Cor. 5:18). What is reconciliation? It is being absolutely joined in one atonement into Christ and being blended with Him in the reconciliation. You are in a glorious place: *"That is, that God was in Christ reconciling the world to Himself, not imputing their trespasses to them, and has committed to us the word of reconciliation"* (v. 19).

Once we are reconciled to Him, we are forever reconciled, made one, brought into conformity. The law of the liberty of the Christ of God reigns supreme over us in all things; that ought to make us leap for joy.

> *Now then, we are ambassadors for Christ, as though God were pleading through us: we implore you on Christ's behalf, be reconciled to God. For He made Him who knew no sin to be sin for us, that we might become the righteousness of God in Him.* (vv. 20–21)

The blessed Son of God has taken our place in reconciliation, becoming the absolute position of all uncleanness, of every sin. God laid upon Him the iniquity of all, so that every iniquity might go, every bondage might be made free. Sin, death, and disease are erased by our resurrection, by our re-creation. When He comes, we will be not naked, but clothed upon, separated, filled within, and made like Him in every way.

## Preparation for the Rapture

I come to you only in the living fact of this realized testimony. To me, it is reality. I am living in it; I am moving in it; I am acting in it; and I am coming to you with the joy of it.

I know this is for us, this divine life, free from bondage, free from the power of Satan, free from evil thoughts, free from thoughts of evil. God reconciles me to Himself in a way that He abounds to me.

It is joy unspeakable and full of glory,
And the half has never yet been told.

Freedom, purity, power, separateness are ours, and we are ready for the Great Trumpet!

Thirteen

# Present-Time Blessings
# for Present-Time Saints

ead with me the first twelve verses of
Matthew 5, the verses that we generally
call the Beatitudes. Some people tell us
that Matthew 5 is a millennial chapter
and that we cannot attain to these blessings at the present time. I believe that everyone who
receives the baptism in the Spirit has a real foretaste
and promise of millennial blessing, but also that here
the Lord Jesus is setting forth present-day blessings
that we can enjoy here and now.

It is a great joy for me to be speaking to baptized
believers. We have not reached the height of God's
mind, but my personal conviction is that we are
nearer by far than we were fourteen years ago. If
anyone had told me that I would be happier today
than I was fourteen years ago when the Lord baptized me in the Spirit, I would not have believed him.
But I see that God has more ahead for us, and that,
so far, we have only touched the fringe of things. As
we let the truth lay hold of us, we will press on for
the goal ahead and enter more fully into our birthright—all that God says.

179

It seems to me that every time I open my Bible I get a new revelation of God's plan. God's Spirit takes man to a place of helplessness and then reveals God as his all in all.

## For the Poor in Spirit

*"Blessed are the poor in spirit, for theirs is the kingdom of heaven"* (Matt. 5:3). This is one of the richest places into which Jesus brings us. The poor have a right to everything in heaven. *"Theirs is."* Do you dare believe it? Yes, I dare. I believe, I know, that I was very poor. When God's Spirit comes in as the ruling, controlling power of our life, He gives us God's revelation of our inward poverty and shows us that God has come with one purpose: to bring heaven's best to earth. He also shows that with Jesus He will indeed *"freely give us all things"* (Rom. 8:32).

An old man and an old woman had lived together for seventy years. Someone said to them, "You must have seen many clouds during those days." They replied, "Where do the showers come from? You never get showers without clouds." It is only the Holy Spirit who can bring us to the place of realization of our poverty; but, every time He does it, He opens the windows of heaven, and the showers of blessing fall.

But I must recognize the difference between my own spirit and the Holy Spirit. My own spirit can do certain things on natural lines—it can even weep and pray and worship—but it is all on a human plane. We must not depend on our own human thoughts and activities or on our own personalities.

## Present-Time Blessings for Present-Time Saints

If the baptism means anything to you, it should bring you to the death of the ordinary, where you are no longer putting faith in your own understanding but, conscious of your own poverty, you are ever yielded to the Spirit. Then it is that your body becomes filled with heaven on earth.

### For Those Who Mourn

*"Blessed are those who mourn, for they shall be comforted"* (Matt. 5:4). People get a wrong idea of mourning. In Switzerland, they have a day set apart to take wreaths to graves. I laughed at the people's ignorance and said, "Why are you spending time around the graves? The people you love are not there. All that taking of flowers to the graves is not faith at all. Those who died in Christ are gone to be with Him, *'which,'* Paul said, *'is far better'* (Phil. 1:23)."

My wife once said to me, "Watch me when I'm preaching. I get so near to heaven when I'm preaching that some day I'll be off." One night she was preaching, and when she had finished, off she went. I was going to Glasgow and had said goodbye to her before she went to the meeting. As I was leaving the house, the doctor and policeman met me at the door and told me that she had fallen dead at the church door. I knew she had gotten what she wanted. I could not weep, but I was in tongues, praising the Lord. On natural lines she was everything to me; but I could not mourn on natural lines, and I just laughed in the Spirit. The house was soon filled with people. The doctor said, "She is dead, and we can do no more for her." I went up to her lifeless corpse and commanded death to give her up, and she came back to me for a moment. Then God said to me, "She is Mine; her work is done." I knew what He meant.

They laid her in the coffin, and I brought my sons and my daughter into the room and said, "Is she there?" They said, "No, Father." I said, "We will cover her up." If you go mourning the loss of loved ones who have gone to be with Christ—I say this to you out of love—you have never had the revelation of what Paul spoke of when he showed us that it is better to go than to stay. We read this in Scripture, but the trouble is that people will not believe it. When you believe God, you will say, "Whatever it is, it is all right. If You want to take the one I love, it is all right, Lord." Faith removes all tears of self-pity.

But there is a mourning in the Spirit. God will bring you to a place where things must be changed, and there is a mourning, an unutterable groaning until God comes. And the end of all real faith always is rejoicing. Jesus mourned over Jerusalem. He saw the conditions; He saw the unbelief; He saw the end of those who closed their ears to the Gospel. But God gave a promise that He would see *"the labor of His soul, and be satisfied"* (Isa. 53:11) and that He would *"see His seed"* (v. 10).

What happened on the Day of Pentecost in Jerusalem was a promise of what would be the results of His travail, to be multiplied a billionfold all down the ages in all the world. And as we enter in the Spirit into travail over conditions that are wrong, such mourning will always bring results for God, and our joy will be complete in the satisfaction that is thereby brought to Christ.

# Present-Time Blessings for Present-Time Saints

## For the Meek

*"Blessed are the meek, for they shall inherit the earth"* (Matt. 5:5). Moses was headstrong in his zeal for his own people, and it resulted in his killing a man. (See Exodus 2:11–12.) His heart was right in his desire to correct things, but he was working on natural lines, and when we work on natural lines we always fail. Moses had a mighty passion, and that is one of the best things in the world when God has control and it becomes a passion for souls to be born again. But apart from God it is one of the worst things.

Paul had it to a tremendous extent, and, breathing out threats, he was sending men and women to prison. (See Acts 8:3.) But God changed him, and later he said he could wish himself accursed from Christ for the sake of his fellowmen, his kinsmen according to the flesh (Rom. 9:3–4).

God took the headstrong Moses and molded him into the meekest of men. He took the fiery Saul of Tarsus and made him the foremost exponent of grace. Oh, brothers and sisters, God can transform you in the same manner, and plant in you a divine meekness and every other thing that you lack.

In our Sunday school, we had a boy with red hair. His head was as red as fire, and so was his temper. He was such a trial. He kicked his teachers and the superintendent. He was simply uncontrollable. The teachers had a meeting in which they discussed the matter of expelling him. But they thought that God might somehow work in that boy, and so they decided to give him another chance. One day he had to be kicked out, and he broke all the windows of the church. He was worse outside than in. Sometime later, we had a ten-day revival meeting. There was nothing much going on in that meeting, and people thought it was a waste of time, but there was one result—the redheaded lad got saved.

After he was saved, the difficulty was to get rid of him at our house. He would be there until midnight, crying to God to make him pliable and use him for His glory. God delivered the lad from his temper and made him one of the meekest, most beautiful boys you ever saw. For twenty years he has been a mighty missionary in China. God takes us just as we are and transforms us by His power.

I can remember the time when I used to go white with rage and shake all over with temper. I could hardly hold myself together. But one time I waited on God for ten days. In those ten days, I was being emptied out, and the life of the Lord Jesus was being worked into me. My wife testified of the transformation that took place in my life. She said, "I never saw such a change. I have never been able to cook anything since that time that has not pleased him. Nothing is too hot or too cold; everything is just right." God must come and reign supreme in your life. Will you let Him do it? He can do it, and He will if you will let Him.

It is no use trying to tame the *"old man"* (Eph. 4:22). But God can deal with him. The carnal mind will never be subjected to God, but God will bring it to the Cross where it belongs and will put in its place, the pure, the holy, the meek mind of the Master.

## For Those Who Hunger and Thirst

*"Blessed are those who hunger and thirst for righteousness, for they shall be filled"* (Matt. 5:6).

## Present-Time Blessings for Present-Time Saints

Note that the verse says, *"Shall be filled."* If you ever see a *"shall"* in the Bible, make it yours. Meet the conditions, and God will fulfill His Word to you. The Spirit of God is crying,

> *Everyone who thirsts, come to the waters; and you who have no money, come, buy and eat. Yes, come, buy wine and milk without money and without price.* (Isa. 55:1)

The Spirit of God will take of the things of Christ and show them to you so that you may have a longing for Christ in His fullness, and when there is that longing, God will not fail to fill you.

See the crowd of worshippers who have come up to the feast. They are going away utterly unsatisfied, but

> *on the last day, that great day of the feast, Jesus* [will stand] *and* [cry] *out, saying, "If anyone thirsts, let him come to Me and drink. He who believes in Me, as the Scripture has said, out of his heart will flow rivers of living water."* (John 7:37–38)

Jesus knows that they are going away without the living water, and so He directs them to the true source of supply. Are you thirsty today? The living Christ still invites you to Himself, and I want to testify that He still satisfies the thirsty soul and still fills the hungry with good things.

In Switzerland, I learned of a man who met with the assembly of the Plymouth Brethren. He attended their various meetings, and one morning, at their Communion service, he arose and said, "Brothers, we have the Word, and I feel that we are living very much in the letter of it, but there is a hunger and thirst in my soul for something deeper, something more real than we have, and I cannot rest until I enter into it." The next Sunday this brother rose again and said, "We are all so poor here, there is no life in this assembly, and my heart is hungry for reality." He did this for several weeks until it got on the nerves of these people, and they protested, "Sands, you are making us all miserable; you are spoiling our meetings. There is only one thing for you to do, and that is to clear out."

That man went out of the meeting in a very sad condition. As he stood outside, one of his children asked him what was the matter, and he said, "To think that they should turn me out from their midst for being hungry and thirsty for more of God!" I did not know anything more of this situation until afterward.

Days later, someone rushed up to Sands and said, "There is a man over here from England, and he is speaking about tongues and healing." Sands said, "I'll fix him. I'll go to the meeting and sit right up in the front and challenge him with the Scriptures. I'll dare him to preach these things in Switzerland. I'll publicly denounce him." So he came to the meetings. There he sat. He was so hungry and thirsty that he drank in every word that was said. His opposition soon petered out. The first morning he said to a friend, "This is what I want." He drank and drank of the Spirit. After three weeks he said, "God will have to do something new or I'll burst." He breathed in God, and the Lord filled him to such an extent that he spoke in other tongues as the

Spirit gave utterance. Sands is now preaching and is in charge of a new Pentecostal assembly.

God is making people hungry and thirsty after His best. And everywhere He is filling the hungry and giving them what the disciples received at the very beginning. Are you hungry? If you are, God promises that you will be filled.

Fourteen

# The Riches of His Glory

ay the Lord of Hosts so surround us with revelation and blessing that our bodies get to the place where they can scarcely contain the joys of the Lord. He will bring us to so rich a place of divine order that forever we will know we are only the Lord's. What a blessed state of grace to be brought into, where we know that the body, the soul, the spirit are preserved blameless until the coming of the Lord! Paul took us one step higher and said, *"May your whole spirit, soul, and body be preserved blameless at the coming of our Lord"* (1 Thess. 5:23). What a blessed state of grace!

When our hearts are moved to believe God, God is greatly desirous for us to have more of His presence. We have only one purpose in mind in these meetings, and that is to strengthen you, to build you up in the most holy faith, and to present you for every good work so that you should be faultless in Him, quickened by the might of the Spirit, so that you might be prepared for everything that God has for you in the future. Our human nature may be brought to a place where it is so superabundantly attended to by God that in the body we will know nothing but the Lord of Hosts.

To this end, I bring you to the banquet that cannot be exhausted, a supply beyond all human thought, an abundance beyond all human extravagances. No matter how you come into great faith and believing in God, God says, "Much more abundantly, much more." So, I trust you will be moved to believe for more.

Are you ready? What for? That you might by the power of God be brought into His coffers with a new plan of righteousness, that you might be able as never before to leave the things of the world behind you and press on toward the prize of the high calling (Phil. 3:13–14).

Are you ready? What for? That you might be so in God's plan that you will feel God's hand upon you. You will know that He has chosen you, so that you might be a firstfruit unto God.

Are you ready? What for? That the Lord will have His choice, that His will and purpose will be yours, that the "Amen" of His character may sweep through your very nature, and that you may know as you have never known before that this is the day of the visitation between you and Him.

## From Human to Divine

The Lord has been speaking to me about this meeting, and I believe we are going to study a Scripture that will be pleasing to Him, the third chapter of Ephesians.

I thank God for this stupendous, glorious exit of human into divine. I praise God for these studies, which are showing us the fullness of the pleasure of God.

It is the God of all grace who is bending over us with the fullness of recognition. He sees us; He knows us; He is acquainted with us. He is bending over us so that His infinite pleasure, His glorious, exhaustless pleasure may move us today. What can please Him more than to see His sons and daughters clothed, in their right mind (see Luke 8:35), listening to His voice, their eyes and ears awake, coming into the treasury of the Most High?

> *For this reason I, Paul, the prisoner of Christ Jesus for you Gentiles; if indeed you have heard of the dispensation of the grace of God which was given to me for you, how that by revelation He made known to me the mystery...which in other ages was not made known to the sons of men, as it has now been revealed by the Spirit to His holy apostles and prophets: that the Gentiles should be fellow heirs, of the same body, and partakers of His promise in Christ through the gospel.*
> (Eph. 3:1–3, 5–6)

Oh, that we might be so clothed upon by the ministry of His grace, that we might so understand the mystery of His wonderful initiative! If only we could comprehend today more than ever before why the Gentiles have been brought into the glories of His treasury, to feed on the finest of the wheat, to drink at the riches of His pleasure, to be filled with the God of love that has no measure.

Without doubt, the greatest mystery of all time from the commencement of creation to now is Christ made manifest in human flesh. What can be greater than eternal life working mightily through eternal death? What can there be greater than the nature and appearance of Adam being changed by a new nature that has to be the fullness of the expression of the Father in heaven? *"And as we have borne the image of the man of dust, we shall also bear the image of the heavenly"* (1 Cor. 15:49).

Everybody recognizes the Adamic race, but may God today let us understand fullness, the divine reflection. May He put us in the glorious position so that we may be changed—the living manifestation of the power of God changing our vestige. May He allow us to see the very expression of the Father, until the terrestrial will pass away, the celestial will come, and the rightness of His glory will press through all our humanity. Heaven will have an exhibition in us that it never before could have, and all the saints will be gathered. The very expression of the Master's face and the very glory of the Father will be in us.

### Interpretation of Tongues

It is the life from heaven that changes what could not be changed. Only the very expression of the nature of the God of all grace moving in our human faculties makes us know that we are begotten from above, changed by His power, transformed by His love, until we are not, for God has taken us. (See Genesis 5:24.)

Be still, for the grace that has come upon you is to so transform your fashion and so beautify your comeliness until right within you there will be the expression of the glory of God in the old creation, making the new creation just longing to depart.

# The Riches of His Glory

Oh, that the breath of heaven would move us today until we would feel, whatever happened, that we must move on to get ready for exit!

## Our Joint Inheritance

The fullness of the expression of the Holy Spirit order today is giving us a glimpse into what has been provided by the Father. We know that in the old Israel, from Abraham right down, God had a very special position. I am speaking now not of the mixed company but of those of whom Jesus said, "Is not this a daughter of Abraham?" (See Luke 13:16.) Paul spoke about it, knowing that he belonged to that royal aristocracy of Abraham's seed.

But the Gentiles had no right to it. The Master said to the Syrophenician woman, "Shall I take the bread of the children and give it to dogs?" (See Mark 7:27.) Did Jesus mean that the Gentiles were dogs? No, He did not mean that, but He meant that the whole race of the Gentiles knew that they were far below the standard and the order of those people who belonged to the royal stock of Israel. The Samaritans all felt it.

"But isn't it possible for the dogs to have some crumbs?" was the woman's question. (See verse 28.)

God has something better than crumbs. God has turned to the Gentiles, and He has made us of the same body, the same heirs. He has put no difference between them and us, but He has joined us up in that blessed order of coming into the promise through the blood of Christ.

Thank God! He met the need of all nations, of all ranks, of all conditions, and God so manifests His power that He has brought us into oneness, and we know we are sharing in the glory. We are sharing in the inner expression; we are sharing that beautiful position in which we know that we belong to the aristocracy of the church of God.

I want to bring you into very blessed privileges along these lines, for I want especially to deal with the knowledge of the inner working of that joint fellowship in this holy order with Christ. *"As it has now been revealed by the Spirit to His holy apostles and prophets"* (Eph. 3:5).

I want you to see that this revelation was given by the power of the Spirit, and I want you to keep in mind that revelations are within the very body where Christ is manifested in the body. When Christ becomes the very personality of the fullness of the Father's will, then the Spirit, the effectual working of the power of God, has such glorious liberty in the body to unfold the mystery and the glories of the kingdom, for it is given to the Holy Spirit to reveal them as He reveals them all in Christ.

It is wonderful to know that I am in the body. It is wonderful to know that the apostles and prophets and all those who have passed down the years, holding aloft the torch, going on from victory to victory, all will be in the body. But how wonderful if we may be in the body so that we might be chosen out of the body to be the bride! It will be according as you are yielded to the *"effective working of His power"* (v. 7).

## Power That Brings Light and Life

*"The effective working of His power"* means to say that it is always Godward. The Holy Spirit has

no alternative; He is here to fulfill the Great Commission of the Executive of heaven. Therefore, He is in the body for one express purpose: to make us understand the fullness of the glories that are contained in what is in us, which is Christ in us—not only the hope of glory (Col. 1:27), but also all the powers of the manifestation of the glory of Christ to be revealed in us.

It is for us to know the mysteries that have been laid up for us. It is for us to know the glories that will be revealed in Christ. It is for us to know all the fullness of the expression of His deity within us. It is for us to know that in this purposing of Christ's being in us, we have to be loosed from everything else, and He has to be manifesting and declaring to us. We have to be subservient, so that He may reign, rule, and have perfect authority, until in the body we are reigning over principalities and powers and every evil thing in the world.

The greatest mystery that has ever been known in the world, or ever will be known, is not only the spiritual body, but it is also the Gospel that has a creative power within it that brings light, liberty, immortality, and life. It is not only that, but it is also that after the seed, which is the life of the Son of God, has been put within you, Christ may be so formed in you that every revelation God has designed is for you because of His divine power in the body.

After the revelation came, after God began speaking to Paul, he felt so unworthy of this that he said, "[I] *am less than the least of all the saints*" (Eph. 3:8). There is nothing but revelation that will take you to humility. If ever it goes the other way, it is because you have never yet under any circumstances been brought to a death like that of Christ.

All lifts, all summits, all glories, all revelation is in the death, when we are so dead to selfishness and self-desire, when we absolutely have been brought to the place of worthlessness and helplessness. Then, in that place, the power of the Holy Spirit works mightily through us.

*"Less than the least of all the saints."* What a blessed state of grace! Paul did not assert himself in any way. It did not matter where he saw the saint, he said, "I am less worthy than that." Oh, what a submission! How the principle of Christ was working through him!

Jesus knew that He was cooperating, perfectly united, that there was not a thing between Him and His Father, so He was in perfect order. Yet He *"made Himself of no reputation"* (Phil. 2:7). He submitted Himself to the Father, and just in the submission of going down, down, down, even to the death of the cross, God said to Him: "Oh, my Son! You are worthy of ten thousand thrones. You are worthy of all I have, and I will give you a name above every name."

There is not a name like the name of Jesus. All through eternity, that name will swing through the great anthems when they bring all the singers and all the angels, and there will be one song above all, *"To Him who loved us"* (Rev. 1:5).

May that make you the least of all saints, make you feel, "How can I submit myself to God so He can have royal preeminence, so that I will not refer to myself but He will be glorified?"

## The Riches of His Glory

Isn't Jesus lovely? It pleased the Father to give Him the place. Nothing but humility will do it. Always be careful when you begin bouncing about, thinking you are somebody. More grace means more death to self; more life means more submission; more revelation means more baseness.

Why? That the excellency of the power, of the light, of the glory, may be exhibited. It is not I, but Another.

And thus it is proper for Christ to fulfill all righteousness in our human bodies, so that we may come to a place where we cease to be, for God's Son has to be royal; He has to be all and in all.

> All in all! All in all!
> Strength in time of weariness,
> A light where shadows fall;
> All in all! All in all!
> Jesus is my all in all.

Christ wants to be glorified right in your mortal bodies, so that there will be a manifestation of this very revelation of Christ in you, the hope, the evidence of eternal glory.

## A Vision of the Church

For what purpose is the church formed together? That the Lord's people should be in the great mystery. Abraham, Isaac, Jacob, and the twelve patriarchs laid wonderful store upon the promise of God, and there was no hope for us Gentiles at all. But they missed the opportunity. They might have gone on to have been the greatest miracle workers, the most profound teachers of the truth. They might have been everywhere, all over the world, bringing such glorious revivals, because they were entrusted to it. But they failed God.

A very few of the apostles—when there was no open door for the Gospel, when their bodies were just filled with luminous light and the power of God pressing them right on—felt sure that that inward power was not meant to be exploded at nothing, so God moved upon them to turn to the Gentiles. Then a special revelation was given to Paul that God had joined up all the Gentiles.

My daughter often speaks of the ebony that will be around the throne because of the Africans who will be there. The Chinese will look very lovely around the throne, too, and the Japanese. All nations, peoples, kindred, and tongues are to be in the great body in heaven—all nationalities, all colors. What a blending of beauty in the glory, when all races will be filled with the glory, every one in its own nationality and yet in the express image of the Father! What a sight!

It is coming. It is already working in the body, and the body is feeling now that we are members in particular. In order that there will be no schism in the body, the Holy Spirit must have a royal place, effectively working through your mind, through your will, through every member of your body, until, as the Word of God says, every part of you is sanctified for the purpose that He may have preeminence. God will work in you, mightily through you, in all ways making manifestation in the human flesh—Christ in you!

# The Riches of His Glory

## Your Part in the Body

You have the vision of the body; now I want you to get the vision of your personality in the body. There is no greater language than this about the Lord, that all fullness dwells in Him. (See Colossians 1:19.) Christ is to be a manifestation in humanity, with all fullness.

Do not be afraid of claiming your right. It is not a measure that you have come to. Remember, John saw Him, and he said that he had a measure that could not be measured. Christ is coming to us with this measure that cannot be measured. Human calculation will not do.

Paul went on to say this remarkable thing: that we may be able to have some revelation of the mightiness of God in its fullness.

> *To me, who am less than the least of all the saints, this grace was given, that I should preach among the Gentiles the unsearchable riches of Christ, and to make all see what is the fellowship of the mystery, which from the beginning of the ages has been hidden in God who created all things through Jesus Christ; to the intent....* (Eph. 3:8–10)

God would have us to understand that those mighty words are to a certain intent. What is the intent?

> *To the intent that now the manifold wisdom of God might be made known by the church to the principalities and powers in the heavenly places.* (Eph. 3:10)

# Smith Wigglesworth on Heaven

The church is rising in all her vision and destroying the powers of darkness, ruling among the powers of wickedness, and transforming darkness to light by the power of the new creation in us. The church is doing all this to the intent that we might know the power that is working in us by the resurrection of the life of Christ.

So we are enriched with all enrichment; we are endued with all beatitudes; we are covered with all the graces; and now we are coming into all the mysteries, that the gifts of the Spirit may be so manifested in us that we might be a constancy of firstfruit.

People are always asking me what I belong to. It makes a lot of difference—they either have plenty of room for your company or not, it all depends where you belong. So I always say, and they do not seem to understand it, "I will give you my credentials, they are right here. I wrote them down so that I would always have them ready. They are, 'T.S.E.W.S.A.'"

"Oh! We never knew there were a people that had such credentials. What are they?"

"The Sect Every Where Spoken Against."

Glory to God! To the intent that this sect everywhere spoken against might be envisioned by an incarnation of glorious authority, Christ is in us mightier than death, mightier than sin, triumphing over principalities and powers.

There can be within you a mighty moving of this intent, of this habitual, divine activity of Christ being manifested in you, which was the revelation of Paul.

The second revelation of Paul, which never from the foundation of the world had been revealed, is that the Son of God, the very embodiment of the nature of the Most High, the very incarnation of His presence and power, could fill a human vessel to its utmost capacity, until the very nature of Him will sweep through by the power of God in the body.

You cannot enter into this without being enlarged, abounding, and superabundant. Everything in God is enlargement. God never wants a child of His in the world to be measured. You cannot measure your place. You might measure your land, you might measure your harvest, but you cannot measure the purposes of the Spirit life: they are boundless; they are infinite. They are for the finite, but all the riches of God are infinite and boundless. There is no such thing as measuring them. If ever you measure God, you will be thin and little and dwarfed. You cannot measure. You have an exhaustless place.

God's Son is in you with all the power of development, until you are so enriched by this divine grace that you live in the world knowing that God is transforming you from grace to grace, from victory to victory.

The Spirit in you has no other foundation than from glory unto glory. Paul was so enlarged in the Spirit in this third chapter of Ephesians that his language failed to go on. And then, when he failed to go on in his language, he bowed his knees unto the Father. Oh, this is supreme! This is beyond all that could be! When language failed, when prophecy had no more room, it seems that he came to a place where he got down on his knees. Then we hear by the power of the Spirit language beyond all Paul could ever say: *"For this reason I bow my knees to the Father of our*

# Smith Wigglesworth on Heaven

*Lord Jesus Christ, from whom the whole family in heaven and earth is named"* (Eph. 3:14–15).

Paul realized that he was joining earth and heaven together. They are one, thank God! There is nothing between us and heaven. Gravity may hold us, but all in heaven and in earth are joined under one blood, with no division or separation. *"To be absent from the body* [is] *to be present with the Lord"* (2 Cor. 5:8).

## More Than What You Expect

God has something here for us in the language of the Holy Spirit. He wants it to enlarge our hearts and take a breath of heaven. Let your whole soul reach out unto God; dare to breathe in heaven; dare to be awakened to all God's mind; listen to the language of the Holy Spirit. Paul was praying in the Spirit:

> *That He would grant you, according to the riches of His glory, to be strengthened with might through His Spirit in the inner man, that Christ may dwell in your hearts through faith; that you, being rooted and grounded in love, may be able to comprehend with all the saints what is the width and length and depth and height; to know the love of Christ which passes knowledge; that you may be filled with all the fullness of God. Now to Him who is able to do exceedingly abundantly above all that we ask or think, according to the power that works in us, to Him be glory in the church by Christ Jesus to all generations, forever and ever. Amen.* (Eph. 3:16–21)

# The Riches of His Glory

This is the Gentile's inhabitation; this is the Gentile's position; this is the body that is being joined up—this spiritual body that has to come into a fullness beyond all expectations.

You cannot expect the fullness that He has waiting for you. If you cannot think of it, then I am sure you cannot expect it. If you cannot ask, then I am sure it is larger than you can expect.

The Holy Spirit takes these things and brings them before us this morning, to the intent that this wonderful, divine appointment will be ours.

How may I get nearer to God? How may I be in the place of helplessness—in my own place and dependent on God? I see a tide rising. *"Blessed are the poor in spirit, for theirs is the kingdom of heaven"* (Matt. 5:3). God is making us very poor, but we are rich in it because our hands are stretched out toward Him in this holy day of His visitation to our hearts.

Believe that He is in you. Believe that He is almightiness. Believe that He is all fullness. Then let yourself go until He is on the throne of your heart. Let everything submit itself to God's throne and the King. Yield yourself unto Him in so sublime a position that He is in perfect order over everything. Let God have His perfect way through you. If you will let go, God will take hold and keep you up.

Oh, to seek only the will of God, to be only in the purpose of God, to seek only that God will be glorified, and not I! We need to repeat the words over and over in our hearts: "Not I, but Christ." (See Galatians 2:20.)

How did it come to Paul? It came when he was *"less than the least of all the saints"* (Eph. 3:8). The effective working of the power when he was *"less than the least of all the saints"* buoyed him up until God was manifested in that mortal flesh, for surely Paul reached into all the fullness of that mighty God.

I believe God wants to send you away filled with the Spirit. Oh, beloved, are you ready? What must you do? You must say, "Father, have your way. Do not let my human will spoil your divine plan. Father, take charge of me today in such a way that I will be wholly, entirely on the altar for Your service." And I am sure He will meet you in this.

Fifteen

# The Glory of the Incorruptible

od has wonderful things for us in this present tense. I wish to enlarge your capacity of thought and also your inward desire toward God, so that you may richly claim all the things God has for you today.

God has, from before the foundation of the world, made a provision for us all, and many are coming into the knowledge that they have been pre-thought about, predestined, and wonderfully changed in the operation of the Spirit.

Are you ready? What for? To obtain the strength of God by a living faith.

Be ready for the enduement of power (Luke 24:49), the enrichment of His grace, the oil that causes you to rejoice and be glad. Be full of expectation; be earnest; make your supplications without fear; be bold in the presence of God; dare to believe that you enter in through the blood into a very large place today.

Are you ready? What for? That you may be lost in God, wholly swallowed up in His divine plan; that you might be enriched above all enrichment of

205

earthly things with divine capacity, with the knowledge of His sovereign grace, so that you may be filled with all His fullness.

## A Supernatural Order

Our subject this morning belongs to the deep things of God. In these days, we need to be grounded in an inward knowledge of greater things. We need to be supernaturally built, changed by a living authority, to come into a divine construction where the mind is operated by the spirit and where we live because Another mightier than us lives in us.

Oh, for a revelation that we may be taken on with God—not left behind, but taken on with God into all His divine arrangement for us! This meeting, however beautiful it may be, is all arranged, divinely arranged. There is nothing out of order with God. God is so large in all of His providences; He is providing, arranging, so that these meetings are not just happening. God has had these in His perfect order.

Occasionally I see one of my hairs fall out of my head, but God knows the number that are left. I am not troubled about my hair, whether it grows white or remains its natural color. Some people try to change the color of their hair. They have forgotten that God has said you cannot make one hair black or white (Matt. 5:36).

We ought to see that God wants us in a supernatural order, not conformed to the world, with all kinds of make-up or fancy garments. Don't you know that you have to be pretty in the sight of the Lord, that prettiness is a meek and quiet spirit? It is where the Lord has the right-of-way of your heart. It is

where you are not troubled about the natural physique, knowing that the supernatural physique is
being made like Him. We have borne the image of
the earthly, but we are going to bear the image of the
heavenly (1 Cor. 15:49).

Oh, that we could be lost to these things, set
apart for the glory of God, brought into the resurrection order, filled with audacity! This is our divine
appointment, where the Lord is taking us on.
Heights, depths, lengths, breadths, yes, everything
in the mind of God—we are being taken higher,
higher, higher!

For our study this morning, I want to take the
first chapter of the first epistle of Peter. This chapter
has a foundation line of truth. We cannot cover it all,
but I want to deal with the incorruptible Word, the
incorruptible seed, and the incorruptible life in the
body, which are all based on an incorruptible plan, so
that you may be able to understand how the mind of
the Lord has to be so extravagantly in you, even to
deny your own personality before you deny the
power of the Word of the living God.

The days will come when your ministry and your
own life will be tested on all lines. If you can get beyond your nature, beyond your natural line of
thought, and beyond yourself into a plane of almighty provision for you in the flesh, quickened by
the Spirit, you will survive. It will be as the Word of
God says, *"Having done all...stand"* (Eph. 6:13).
When the trial is on, when everything comes to a
point where it seems it is the last strand in the rope,
then the Lord will very mightily bring you into a
land of plenty. Lord, let it please You to keep us in
that place.

# Smith Wigglesworth on Heaven

In order to reach this climax in divine order, let us read the beginning of the first epistle of Peter: *"Peter, an apostle of Jesus Christ, to the pilgrims of the Dispersion in Pontus, Galatia, Cappadocia, Asia, and Bithynia"* (1 Pet. 1:1).

Peter, like James, was speaking to us on this line because of a trying time. James was edifying us in a trying corner to remain steadfast. Here we have the same thing.

## Persecution Comes after Baptism

The people were scattered, and persecution had come in. They had had a good time at Jerusalem, and God knew—I say it reverently—God knows that we never make progress in an easy time. You may settle down in your ease and miss the great plan of God. God allowed strange things to happen in Jerusalem after the Holy Spirit came.

A man may be saved for many years without knowing much of anything about persecution. A man may be sanctified for many years without knowing much of anything about persecution. But it is impossible to be baptized with the Holy Spirit without entering into persecution.

The disciples had a wonderful time when they were with Jesus. They had no persecution, but there was One in the midst of them whom the people of Nazareth tried to throw over the brow of the hill. The priests joined together to kill Him.

After the devil entered into Judas, the only people he could have conversation with were the priests. The priests were willing to talk to the devil after he got into Judas.

# The Glory of the Incorruptible

## Interpretation of Tongues

Guard the door of your lips; see to it that your heart is perfect, that you have no judgment, that you do not stand in the way and condemn everybody that is in the way, for there are many today who are like the priests in their day: they will neither go in themselves nor let anybody else go in (Matt. 23:13). But don't let this spirit be in you, for God wants to guard you, purify you, and present you as a chaste virgin, made ready for every good work.

Let us see to it, whatever happens, that there is no harsh judgment in us, no bitterness. We must see that we have been quickened, brought into, changed by a new authority, incorruptible in the corruptible. We must see that we have the divine life where death was, love where hatred was, the power of God reigning in the human, the Lord lifting upon us the light of His countenance right in the midst of death, and life breaking forth like rivers in the desert.

May the Lord bring us to a place in which hard judgment is past. May He make us meek and lowly in heart. This is the principle of the Master.

## Satan Cannot Be Made Holy

There is no such thing as purifying the impure. Evil things never get purer, but more vile. All impurity, all evil must be cast out. You can never make Satan holy. He will be hellish and fiendish forever, and when the brightness of God comes by the express image of the Father, the very brightness against uncleanness, he will be glad to get in the pit and be there forever and ever.

# Smith Wigglesworth on Heaven

There are some fools in this day who foolishly say that the devil will be saved, and that they will go arm in arm with him. It is because they do not rightly understand the Word of God. You will never purify sin. Sin cannot be purified. *"The carnal mind...is not subject to the law of God, nor indeed can be"* (Rom. 8:7). Carnality has to be destroyed. Evil propensities must be rooted out.

God's plan is, "I will give you a pure heart and a right spirit." And this is the order of the new creation in God.

As surely as the Holy Spirit fell, James was beheaded, Peter was put in prison, they had a tremendous trouble at Jerusalem, and the saints were scattered. The scattering of the saints meant the proclamation of the Gospel. So here Peter was writing to the people who had been scattered.

## Sanctification of the Human Spirit

*Elect according to the foreknowledge of God the Father, in sanctification of the Spirit, for obedience and sprinkling of the blood of Jesus Christ: Grace to you and peace be multiplied.*
(1 Pet. 1:2)

Notice that there is a sanctifying of the human spirit. It does not matter what you say, if your human spirit does not get wholly sanctified, you will always be in danger. It is that position where the devil has a chance to work upon you. Therefore, we are taught to come into sanctification where uncleannesses and corruption pass away because of incorruption abiding, where all kinds of lusts have lost their power.

# The Glory of the Incorruptible

This is the plan. Only in the ideal of pursuit of this does God so bless us in our purifying state that we lose our position because of the ascended position with Him in the glory. The saints of God, as they go on into perfection and holiness and understand the mind of the Spirit and the law of the spirit of life, are brought into a very blessed place.

For instance, it is the place of holiness, the place of entire sanctification, the place where God has the throne of the heart. It is the place where the mind is so concentrated in the power of God that a person thinks about the things that are pure and lives in holy ascendancy, where every day is an exchange into the power of freedom with God. God highly honors him, but He never exalts him. The devil comes to exalt him, but it cannot be under the lines of the sanctification of the spirit.

There is a sanctifying of the human spirit during which the human spirit comes into such perfect blending with the divine mind of Christ that the person cannot be exalted. You can live in the body with glorious anointing, revelation, and power. The Spirit can sanctify your spirit until you will never vaunt yourself and will never say "I, I, I," but it will be "Christ, Christ, Christ." Then Christ will be glorified.

## Interpretation of Tongues

Into this death within, this inward deepening of all human weaknesses and human powers that would assert themselves, deeper, deeper into and on with God, learning only the principles of Christ, as He is, to be like Him in holiness, in righteousness and in purity, until you reign with Him, gloriously reigning in Him, through Him, by Him, over the powers of Satan.

Holiness is power; sin is defeat. Sin is weakness; holiness is strength.

*"Renewed in the spirit of your mind"* (Eph. 4:23) is a place where you are always being lifted into clearer light, always seeing more the hideousness of sin, always having a consciousness of the powers of evil and a consciousness of the powers of God over evil. So may the Lord grant unto us by His mighty power this spiritual intuition of divine association with the Father.

### Interpretation of Tongues

He is exalted far above all, and we are united in Him, closer than all, until there is no division. Holy as He is, pure as He is, life, truth revealed in us. Because of truth in us, He becomes Alpha, Omega; He has the last thought: He is all in all. We love Him! We say, *"He is altogether lovely"* (Song 5:16).

### The Incorruptible Seed

Now consider 1 Peter 1:13–16:

*Therefore gird up the loins of your mind, be sober, and rest your hope fully upon the grace that is to be brought to you at the revelation of Jesus Christ; as obedient children, not conforming yourselves to the former lusts, as in your ignorance; but as He who called you is holy, you also be holy in all your conduct, because it is written, "Be holy, for I am holy."*

It is settled in the canon of Scripture that what came into you at the new birth had no corruption in it, had no defilement in it, and could not desire evil. That incorruptible seed, that divine life of the Son, that quickening of the Spirit, that regenerative power, that holy creative force within you, that divine position—all of these caused your very nature to bring forth a likeness to the Son of God. Even your very organs yearned with desire after its purity; you loved to sing of His holiness.

I remember, when I was a little boy, I used to lie on my back singing until heaven seemed to be let down, until it seemed like glory. It was wonderful! What was it? It was the new creation, longing, waiting. Oh, hallelujah! That was sixty years ago, and I have still greater desire and more longing for what came then to be met with the very life that gave it. There is something so remarkable about it, and it was so concentrated in my human life, that from that day to this, I have never lost that holy knowledge that I am His, wholly His.

I want all of you to be created anew after this fashion until you will become saints: holy, purified, and perfect. Don't be afraid of being called saints; don't be afraid of the word *holiness*; don't be afraid of the word *purified*; don't be afraid of the word *perfect*. Believe that in you there is a power that has no corruption in it, that has no desire to sin, that hates uncleanness, that is born of an incorruptible power, that has no evil in it. It is Godlike, it is sonship order, and it has to grow up in you until He is perfectly manifested in you—perfect sight in God, perfect feeling after God, holy feelings, no carnal desires, yearning after purity, longing after cleanliness, desiring after God. This is the inheritance of the saints: in the world, not of it, but over it.

He who has this faith, he who has this life, overcomes the world. *"Who is he who overcomes the world, but he who believes that Jesus is the Son of God?"* (1 John 5:5).

What does it mean for Him to be the Son of God to you and me? God is holy; God is light; God is love. Jesus was the fullness of the expression of the purpose of all fullness. The same fullness, the same life, the same maturity after the perfect standard of life has to be in you until you are dead indeed to the world and alive to God in the Spirit (Rom. 6:11).

> Holy, Holy, Holy, merciful and mighty,
> God in Three Persons, blessed Trinity.

Trinity, boundless affinity; holy, transforming power—such is the very nature of the Son of God, the very power of the world to come, the very nature of the wonderful Son, formed in us.

There are five senses in the world. When He is come, there are five senses of spiritual acquaintance: the hearing of faith, the feelings after God, the seeing supernaturally, the speaking after the mind of the operation of the Spirit, and the tasting after God's plan.

Yet God wants us to be so triune, perfectly joined, until Christ is formed in us with His very life manifested in the human, until we know we have no questions, no matter what other people say. We know in whom we have believed (2 Tim. 1:12).

There are things that can be moved, and there are things that cannot be moved; there are things that can be changed, and there are things that cannot be changed. We have within us an incorruptible place that cannot be moved. It does not matter who is moved or what is moved; the things that God has given us remain.

Some things can be wrapped up and folded like a garment. The heavens may be rolled up like a scroll (Isa. 34:4) and melt with fervent heat (2 Pet. 3:10). The very earth we are standing on may be absolutely melted. But we are as endurable as He is, for we have the same life, the incorruptible life, the eternal power. The everlasting King is moving in the natural things to cause the natural to know that this is eternal, this is divine, this is God. Hallelujah!

## An Inheritance of Righteousness

Seeing that these things are so, we must build in this order, for it is in this order that nothing can contaminate us. You are perfect over sin, if you will believe it. You are perfect over disease, if you will believe it. You are perfect over death, if you will believe it. You are perfect in the order of Enoch's translation, if you dare believe it.

There are always three things that are working silently but powerfully: the blade, the head, and the full grain in the head (Mark 4:28). God is developing us in a righteous line to know that we are of a royal aristocracy (1 Pet. 2:9); we belong to a new company; we belong to the firstborn; we have the nature of the Son; we belong to eternal workings. God, who is greater than all, has come through all and is now working in all to His glory, to His power.

You may not be able to take these things in because you know so much about gravity, and I am speaking so much about gravity being removed.

There is no gravity to the spirit. There is no gravity to thought. There is no gravity to inspiration. There is no gravity to divine union with Christ. It is above all; it rises higher; it sits on the throne; it claims its purposes.

God has brought us to a place where all manner of evil powers are subdued. Reigning over them, being enriched by the new creation of God in the Spirit, you are not timid and afraid; you meet these things with joy, and you triumph over them in the place of blessing.

Some of you may say, "If I could talk to you about this, I would have to say so many things that I know are in me that are not in that." You must allow the Lord to move you out and bring you into that. Unbelief is the great dethroning place; faith is the great rising place. Many people lose great confidence in the spirit and cease to go on to perfection because they allow their own minds and lives, their own knowledge, their own associations, to continually bring then into a deplorable, low estate.

God says you are not of this world (John 15:19); you have been delivered from the corruption of the world (2 Pet. 1:4); you are being *"transformed by the renewing of your mind"* (Rom. 12:2). God says that you are *"a royal priesthood,"* a holy people (1 Pet. 2:9), belonging to the building of which Christ is the great cornerstone (Eph. 2:20).

The Holy Spirit is coming forth to help you to claim your inheritance. Do not be afraid of getting rich this hour, but be afraid of not coming into your inheritance. Do not be afraid of coming in, but be very afraid if you do not come in. Have God's mind on this: God says you have to overcome the world, that you have to have this incorruptible, undefiled position now within the human body, transforming your mind, even your very nature, realizing the supernatural power working through you.

It is lovely for me to be here speaking about this knowledge of this glorious incarnation of the Spirit, and I want you to know I would be the last man to speak about these things unless I knew they could be attained. This is our inheritance; this is where God wants to make you His own in such a way that you will deny yourself, the flesh, and the world so that you may rule over principalities and powers and over spiritual wickedness in high places (Eph. 6:12), so that you may *"reign in life"* (Rom. 5:17) by this lovely place in Christ Jesus.

## Supernatural Fullness

I want to stir you up today. If I cannot make a person who is suffering from disease righteously indignant against that condition, I cannot help him. If I can make every sufferer know that suffering, disease, and all these things are the workings of the devil, I can help him.

Let me give you a Scripture for it: *"The thief does not come except to steal, and to kill, and to destroy"* (John 10:10). That is the devil. And if you know that, believe the other side of the story, that Jesus has come to give you life, life eternal and life abounding (v. 10).

If you can see that the devil is after you, to kill you for all he is worth, believe that Christ is enthroned in your heart to destroy the very principles of the devil in every way. Have the reality of this;

build upon it by perfect soundness until you are in the place of perfect bliss, for to know Him is perfect bliss. Be so built in Him that you are not afraid of what comes on the line of all evil. You must have a fullness that presses out beyond; you must have a life that is full of divine power; you must have a mind that is perfectly Christ; you must cease to be natural and begin to be supernatural.

God is on His throne and can take you a thousand miles in a moment. Have faith to jump into His supernatural plan.

Are you ready? What for? To be so changed by the order of God that you will never have this human order of fear anymore. Remember that *"perfect love casts out fear"* (1 John 4:18).

Step into the full tide of the life of the manifestation of God. Your new nature has no corruption in it. Eternal life is not just during your lifetime; it is forever. You are regenerated by the power of the Word of God, and it is in you as an incorruptible force, taking you on from victory to victory until death itself can be overcome, until sin has no authority, until disease could not be in the body. This is a living fact by the Word of God.

You may say, "How can I come into this full manifestation?" Read carefully the first two verses of Romans 8:

> *There is therefore now no condemnation to those who are in Christ Jesus, who do not walk according to the flesh, but according to the Spirit. For the law of the Spirit of life in Christ Jesus has made me free from the law of sin and death.* (Rom. 8:1–2)

# The Glory of the Incorruptible

Right in this present moment, there is *"no condemnation."* This law of the Spirit of life is a law in the body; it is a law of eternity; it is a law of God, a new law. It is not the law of the Ten Commandments, but a law of life in the body, changing you in the body until there is no sin power, no disease power, and no death power.

You who desire to go a thousand miles through faith, beyond what you have ever gone before, leap into it. Believe the blood of Christ makes you clean; believe you have come into resurrection order; believe you are young again. Believe you are young. God will renew your youth. Believe it!

You say, "I will try, anyhow." All right, but trying is an effort, whereas believing is a fact. Don't join the Endeavor Society, but come into the Faith Society, and you will leap into the promises of God, which are *"Yes"* and *"Amen"* (2 Cor. 1:20) to all who believe.

Don't look down your nose and murmur anymore. Have a rejoicing spirit; get the praise of God in your heart; go forth from victory to victory; rise in faith, and believe it. You must not live in yourself; you must live in Christ. *"Set your mind on things above"* (Col. 3:2), and keep your whole spirit alive in God. Let your inheritance be so full of divine life that you live above the world and all its thoughts and cares.

## A Prayer

O Lord, move away disease, move away blind eyes, move away imperfect vision. Give the Word; let us understand the blood; let us understand the spirit of prophecy and of testimony. Let us understand, O

God, that You are still building the foundation on the prophets and on the apostles and on all who work Your wonderful Word. Build us in this fashion until every soul is filled with divine grace.

## Questions Answered

**Q:** Is the baptism of the Holy Spirit essential to the Rapture?

**A:** No. It is a good thing to be baptized with the Holy Spirit because—and it is a wonderful thing to me—when the church goes, the Holy Spirit is not here anymore. So it appears that the Holy Spirit goes with the church. The Word of God says that He will bring with Him all who are asleep in Jesus. And there are thousands asleep in Jesus who were never baptized in the Holy Spirit, but He is going to bring them. So it is evident they are there.

Verses sixteen and eighteen of Luke 22 will help you: *"For I say to you, I will no longer eat of it until it is fulfilled in the kingdom of God....For I say to you, I will not drink of the fruit of the vine until the kingdom of God comes."* Jesus said, *"The kingdom of God is within you"* (Luke 17:21). He meant the new creation; He meant the new deposit of life that He had given, for He was and is the life of the world. It would be impossible, He said, for Him to eat or drink again until the kingdom was come.

Every person who has the kingdom of God within him will be there at the Rapture. The Bible doesn't say anything about the baptism; it says the kingdom will be presented at the Supper.

The baptism of the Holy Spirit is for revelation. The baptism of the Holy Spirit is to take the things of Jesus and reveal them. The baptism of the Holy Spirit is to be a focus.

Suppose you put a great magnifying glass onto the smallest thing. What would happen? The Holy Spirit is the great Magnifier of the life, the gifts, and the ministry of the King. And the King, when the Holy Spirit comes, is coronated. Coronation implies that when the Holy Spirit comes into the body, Jesus becomes King, and the Holy Spirit becomes the revealer of kingship.

**Q:** Is the church going through tribulation?
**A:** We have a clear teaching in Thessalonians about the Rapture, and it clearly says, *"Only He who now restrains will do so until He is taken out of the way"* (2 Thess. 2:7).

As sure as anything, the devil is having power given to him at this day and will have more power given to him until he is manifested, right up until he has full liberty and becomes the prince of the earth. At the same time, there is increasing velocity and divine power and quickening and revelation of the saints. Today we are in a day of revelation of the Holy Spirit that possibly has never been. This is the great open door of ministry, and as He is letting in that power, He is filling us with power.

If you are ready for translation, you are ready for anything.

**Q:** Will the bride be taken out after we get to glory?
**A:** Yes, the bride is in the body of Christ. She will not be seen until just before her marriage to Christ; until then, she will be veiled. Even now, God is quickening many people in a remarkable way, and

they are bringing themselves to the place where they will pay the price for holiness and separation. This is intensely the desire of the bridal position.

Now, don't take it that you are in the bride because of this, but prove yourself worthy to be in the body, so that you might be worthy to be taken out of the body as the bride. But don't get ideas about it, because many people are being tremendously fooled, believing that they had within them a manifestation of the bride. That is absolute foolishness. The bride will be taken out right in the kingdom.

**Q:** Will there be anyone saved on the earth after the church is taken away?

**A:** The 144,000 who are perfectly Jewish. They will go through great tribulation because of the Word, and the people, if they are saved at all, will be saved by the Word, not by the Spirit. The Holy Spirit will have gone with the church body. But the 144,000 will be Jewish. They know the Word, and they will go through by the Word. They will even die for the Word.

## The Power of Faith
*Smith Wigglesworth*

Need a miracle? God has one for you.
Trapped in poverty? Access God's unlimited resources.
Lack vision and purpose? Discover your God-given destiny.
Feel powerless? God wants to use you in amazing ways.

Laughing at the impossible was a way of life for Smith Wigglesworth.
He trusted wholeheartedly in the words of Jesus, "Only believe."
God used a simple faith to restore sight to the blind, health to the
sick, even life to the dead. This same kind of miracle-working faith
can be yours. As you believe God, your faith will explode.
Your miracle is waiting for you—dare to believe.

ISBN: 0-88368-608-2 • Trade • 544 pages

**W**
WHITAKER
HOUSE

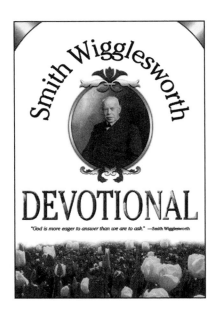

## Smith Wigglesworth Devotional
### Smith Wigglesworth

You are invited to journey with Smith Wigglesworth on a year-long trip that will quench your spiritual thirst while it radically transform your faith. As you daily explore these challenging insights from the Apostle of Faith, you will connect with God's glorious power, cast out doubt, and see impossibilities turn into realities. Your prayer life will never be the same again when you personally experience the joy of seeing awesome, powerful results as you extend God's healing grace to others.

ISBN: 0-88368-574-4 • Trade • 560 pages

---

WHITAKER
HOUSE

proclaiming the power of the Gospel through the written word
visit our website at www.whitakerhouse.com